Bloom's BioCritiques

Bloom's BioCritiques

EUDORA WELTY

Edited and with an introduction by
Harold Bloom
Sterling Professor of the Humanities
Yale University

CHELSEA HOUSE
PUBLISHERS
A Haights Cross Communications Company

Philadelphia

Library of Congress Cataloging-in-Publication Data
Applied for.
ISBN: 0-7910-7870-1

Chelsea House Publishers
1974 Sproul Road, Suite 400
Broomall, PA 19008-0914

http://www.chelseahouse.com

Contributing editor: Samuel Arkin
Cover design by Keith Trego
Cover: © Hulton | Archive by Getty Images, Inc.
Layout by EJB Publishing Services

All links and web addresses were checked and verified to be correct at the time
of publication. Because of the dynamic nature of the web, some addresses and
links may have changed since publication and may no longer be valid.

CONTENTS

USER'S GUIDE

These volumes are designed to introduce the reader to the life and work of the world's literary masters. Each volume begins with Harold Bloom's essay "The Work in the Writer" and a volume-specific introduction also written by Professor Bloom. Following these unique introductions is an engaging biography that discusses the major life events and important literary accomplishments of the author under consideration.

Furthermore, each volume includes an original critique that not only traces the themes, symbols, and ideas apparent in the author's works, but strives to put those works into a cultural and historical perspective. In addition to the original critique is a brief selection of significant critical essays previously published on the author and his or her works followed by a concise and informative chronology of the writer's life. Finally, each volume concludes with a bibliography of the writer's works, a list of additional readings, and an index of important themes and ideas.

HAROLD BLOOM

The Work in the Writer

Literary biography found its masterpiece in James Boswell's *Life of Samuel Johnson*. Boswell, when he treated Johnson's writings, implicitly commented upon Johnson as found in his work, even as in the great critic's life. Modern instances of literary biography, such as Richard Ellmann's lives of W.B. Yeats, James Joyce, and Oscar Wilde, essentially follow in Boswell's pattern.

That the writer somehow is in the work, we need not doubt, though with William Shakespeare, writer-of-writers, we almost always need to rely upon pure surmise. The exquisite rancidities of the Problem Plays or Dark Comedies seem to express an extraordinary estrangement of Shakespeare from himself. When we read or attend *Troilus and Cressida* and *Measure for Measure*, we may be startled by particular speeches of Ulysses in the first play, or of Vincentio in the second. These speeches, of Ulysses upon hierarchy or upon time, or of Duke Vincentio upon death, are too strong either for their contexts or for the characters of their speakers. The same phenomenon occurs with Parolles, the military impostor of *All's Well That Ends Well*. Utterly disgraced, he nevertheless affirms: "Simply the thing I am / Shall make me live."

In Shakespeare, more even than in his peers, Dante and Cervantes, meaning always starts itself again through excess or overflow. The strongest of Shakespeare's creatures—Falstaff, Hamlet, Iago, Lear, Cleopatra—have an exuberance that is fiercer than their plays can contain. If Ben Jonson was at all correct in his complaint that "Shakespeare wanted art," it could have been only in a sense that he may not have intended. Where do the personalities of Falstaff or Hamlet touch a limit? What was it in Shakespeare that made *Hamlet* and the two parts of *Henry IV* into "plays unlimited"? Neither Falstaff nor Hamlet will be stopped: their wit, their beautiful, laughing speech, their intensity of being—all these are virtually infinite.

In what ways do Falstaff and Hamlet manifest the writer in the work? Evidently, we can never know, or know enough to answer with any authority. But what would happen if we reversed the question, and asked: How did the work form the writer, Shakespeare?

Of Shakespeare's inwardness, his biography tells us nothing. And yet, to an astonishing extent, Shakespeare created our inwardness. At the least, we can speculate that Shakespeare so lived his life as to conceal the depths of his nature, particularly as he rather prematurely aged. We do not have Shakespeare on Shakespeare, as any good reader of the Sonnets comes to realize: they do not constitute a key that unlocks his heart. No sequence of sonnets could be less confessional or more powerfully detached from the poet's self.

The German poet and universal genius, Goethe, affords a superb contrast to Shakespeare. Of Goethe's life, we know more than everything; I wonder sometimes if we know as much about Napoleon or Freud or any other human being who ever has lived, as we know about Goethe. Everywhere, we can find Goethe in his work, so much so that Goethe seems to crowd the writing out, just as Byron and Oscar Wilde seem to usurp their own literary accomplishments. Goethe, cunning beyond measure, nevertheless invested a rival exuberance in his greatest works that could match his personal charisma. The sublime outrageousness of the Second Part of *Faust*, or of the greater lyric and meditative poems, forms a Counter-Sublime to Goethe's own daemonic intensity.

Goethe was fascinated by the daemonic in himself; we can doubt that Shakespeare had any such interests. Evidently, Shakespeare abandoned his acting career just before he composed *Measure for Measure* and *Othello*. I surmise that the egregious interventions by Vincentio and Iago displace the actor's energies into a new kind of mischief-making, a fresh opening to a subtler playwriting-within-the-play.

But what had opened Shakespeare to this new awareness? The answer is the work in the writer, *Hamlet* in Shakespeare. One can go further: it was not so much the play, *Hamlet*, as the character Hamlet, who changed Shakespeare's art forever.

Hamlet's personality is so large and varied that it rivals Goethe's own. Ironically Goethe's Faust, his Hamlet, has no personality at all, and is as colorless as Shakespeare himself seems to have chosen to be. Yet nothing could be more colorful than the Second Part of *Faust*, which is peopled by an astonishing array of monsters, grotesque devils and classical ghosts.

A contrast between Shakespeare and Goethe demonstrates that in each—but in very different ways—we can better find the work in the person, than we can discover that banal entity, the person in the work. Goethe to many of his contemporaries seemed to be a mortal god. Shakespeare, so far as we know, seemed an affable, rather ordinary fellow, who aged early and became somewhat withdrawn. Yet Faust, though Mephistopheles battles for his soul, is hardly worth the trouble unless you take him as an idea and not as a person. Hamlet is nearly every-idea-in-one, but he is precisely a personality and a person.

Would Hamlet be so astonishingly persuasive if his father's ghost did not haunt him? Falstaff is more alive than Prince Hal, who says that the devil haunts him in the shape of an old fat man. Three years before composing the final *Hamlet*, Shakespeare invented Falstaff, who then never ceased to haunt his creator. Falstaff and Hamlet may be said to best represent the work in the writer, because their influence upon Shakespeare was prodigious. W.H. Auden accurately observed that Falstaff possesses infinite energy: never tired, never bored, and absolutely both witty and happy until Hal's rejection destroys him. Hamlet too has infinite energy, but in him it is more curse than blessing.

Falstaff and Hamlet can be said to occupy the roles in Shakespeare's invented world that Sancho Panza and Don Quixote possess in Cervantes's. Shakespeare's plays from 1610 on (starting with *Twelfth Night*) are thus analogous to the Second Part of Cervantes's epic novel. Sancho and the Don overtly jostle Cervantes for authorship in the Second Part, even as Cervantes battles against the impostor who has pirated a continuation of his work. As a dramatist, Shakespeare manifests the work in the writer more indirectly. Falstaff's prose genius is revived in the scapegoating of Malvolio by Maria and Sir Toby Belch, while Falstaff's darker insights are developed by Feste's melancholic wit. Hamlet's intellectual resourcefulness, already deadly, becomes poisonous in Iago and in Edmund. Yet we have not crossed into the deeper abysses of the work in the writer in later Shakespeare.

No fictive character, before or since, is Falstaff's equal in self-trust. Sir John, whose delight in himself is contagious, has total confidence both in his self-awareness and in the resources of his language. Hamlet, whose self is as strong, and whose language is as copious, nevertheless distrusts both the self and language. Later Shakespeare is, as it were, much under the influence both of Falstaff and of Hamlet, but they tug him in opposite directions. Shakespeare's own copiousness of language is well-nigh incredible: a vocabulary in excess of twenty-one thousand words, almost eighteen hundred of which he coined himself. And of his word-hoard, nearly half are used only once each, as though the perfect setting for each had been found, and need not be repeated. Love for language and faith in language are Falstaffian attributes. Hamlet will darken both that love and that faith in Shakespeare, and perhaps the Sonnets can best be read as Falstaff and Hamlet counterpointing against one another.

Can we surmise how aware Shakespeare was of Falstaff and Hamlet, once they had played themselves into existence? *Henry IV, Part I* appeared in six quarto editions during Shakespeare's lifetime; *Hamlet* possibly had four. Falstaff and Hamlet were played again and again at the Globe, but Shakespeare knew also that they were being read, and he must have had contact with some of those readers. What would it have been like to discuss Falstaff or Hamlet with one of their early readers (presumably also part of their audience at the Globe), if you were the creator of such demiurges? The question would seem nonsensical to most Shakespeare scholars, but then these days they tend to be either ideologues or moldy figs. How can we recover the uncanniness of Falstaff and of Hamlet, when they now have become so familiar?

A writer's influence upon himself is an unexplored problem in criticism, but such an influence is never free from anxieties. The biocritical problem (which this series attempts to explore) can be divided into two areas, difficult to disengage fully. Accomplished works affect the author's life, and also affect her subsequent writings. It is simpler for me to surmise the effect of *Mrs. Dalloway* and *To the Lighthouse* upon Woolf's late *Between the Acts*, than it is to relate Clarissa Dalloway's suicide and Lily Briscoe's capable endurance in art to the tragic death and complex life of Virginia Woolf.

There are writers whose lives were so vivid that they seem sometimes to obscure the literary achievement: Byron, Wilde, Malraux, Hemingway. But most major Western writers do not live that exuberantly, and the greatest of all, Shakespeare, sometimes appears to have adopted the personal mask of colorlessness. And yet there are heroes of literature who struggled titanically with their own eras—Tolstoy, Milton, Victor Hugo—who nevertheless matter more for their works than their lives.

There are great figures—Emily Dickinson, Wallace Stevens, Willa Cather—who seem to have had so little of the full intensity of life when compared to the vitality of their work, that we might almost speak of the work in the work, rather than even of the work in a person. Emily Brontë might well be the extreme instance of such a visionary, surpassing William Blake in that one regard.

I conclude this general introduction to a series of literary bio-critiques by stating a tentative formula or principle for gauging the many ways in which the work influences the person and her subsequent, later work. Our influence upon ourselves is always related to the Shakespearean invention of self-overhearing, which I have written about in several other contexts. Life, as well as poetry and prose, is overheard rather than simply heard. The writer listens to herself as though she were somebody else, and the will to change begins to operate. The forces that live in us include the prior work we have done, and the dreams and waking visions that evade our dismissals.

HAROLD BLOOM

Introduction

I

Eudora Welty divides her remarkable brief autobiography, *One Writer's Beginnings*, into three parts: "Listening," "Learning to See," "Finding A Voice." Gentle yet admonitory, these titles instruct us in how to read her stories and novels, a reading that necessarily involves further growth in our sense of inwardness. Certain of her stories never cease their process of journeying deep into interior regions we generally reserve only for personal and experiential memories. Doubtless they differ from reader to reader; for me they include "A Still Moment" and "The Burning."

Mark Twain has had so varied a progeny among American writers that we hardly feel surprise when we reflect that Welty and Hemingway both emerge from *Huckleberry Finn*. All that Welty and Hemingway share as storytellers is Twain's example. Their obsessive American concern is Huck's: the freedom of a solitary joy, intimately allied to a superstitious fear of solitude. Welty's people, like Hemingway's, and like the self-representations of our major poets—Whitman, Dickinson, Stevens, Frost, Eliot, Hart Crane, R.P. Warren, Roethke, Elizabeth Bishop, Ashbery, Merrill, and Ammons—all secretly believe themselves to be no part of the creation and all feel free only when they are quite alone.

In *One Writer's Beginning:*, Welty comments upon "A Still Moment":

"A Still Moment"—another early story—was a fantasy, in which the separate interior visions guiding three highly individual and widely differing men marvelously meet and converge upon the same single exterior object. All my characters were actual persons who had lived at the same time, who would have been strangers to one another, but whose lives had actually taken them at some point to the same neighborhood. The scene was in the Mississippi wilderness in the historic year 1811—"*anno mirabilis*," the year the stars fell on Alabama and lemmings, or squirrels perhaps, rushed straight down the continent and plunged into the Gulf of Mexico, and an earthquake made the Mississippi River run backwards and New Madrid, Missouri, tumbled in and disappeared. My real characters were Lorenzo Dow the New England evangelist, Murrell the outlaw bandit and murderer on the Natchez Trace, and Audubon the painter; and the exterior object on which they all at the same moment set their eyes is a small heron, feeding.

Welty's choices—Lorenzo Dow, James Murrell, Audubon—are all obsessed solitaries. Dow, the circuit rider, presumably ought to be the least solipsistic of the three, yet his fierce cry as he rides on at top speed—"I must have souls! And souls I must have!"—is evidence of an emptiness that never can be filled:

> It was the hour of sunset. All the souls that he had saved and all those he had not took dusky shapes in the mist that hung between the high banks, and seemed by their great number and density to block his way, and showed no signs of melting or changing back into mist, so that he feared his passage was to be difficult forever. The poor souls that were not saved were darker and more pitiful than those that were, and still there was not any of the radiance he would have hoped to see in such a congregation.

As Dow himself observes, his eyes are in a "failing proportion to my loving heart always," which makes us doubt his heart. He loves his wife, Peggy, effortlessly since she is in Massachusetts and he is galloping along on the Old Natchez Trace. Indeed, their love can be altogether effortless, consisting as it does of a marriage proposal, accepted as his first words to her, a few hours of union, and his rapid departure south for evangelical purposes, pursued by her first letter declaring that she, like her husband, fears only death, but never mere separation.

This remarkable hunter of souls, intrepid at evading rapacious Indians or Irish Catholics, can be regarded as a sublime lunatic, or merely as a pure product of America:

> Soon night would descend, and a camp-meeting ground ahead would fill with its sinners like the sky with its stars. How he hungered for them! He looked in prescience with a longing of love over the throng that waited while the flames of the torches threw change, change, change over their faces. How could he bring them enough, if it were not divine love and sufficient warning of all that could threaten them? He rode on faster. He was a filler of appointments, and he filled more and more, until his journeys up and down creation were nothing but a shuttle, driving back and forth upon the rich expanse of his vision. He was homeless by his own choice, he must be everywhere at some time, and somewhere soon. There hastening in the wilderness on his flying horse he gave the night's torch-lit crowd a premature benediction, he could not wait. He spread his arms out, one at a time for safety, and he wished, when they would all be gathered in by his tin horn blasts and the inspired words would go out over their heads, to brood above the entire and passionate life of the wide world, to become its rightful part.
>
> He peered ahead. "Inhabitants of Time! The wilderness is your souls on earth!" he shouted ahead into the treetops. "Look about you, if you would view the conditions of your spirit, put here by the good Lord to show you and afright you. These wild places and these trails of awesome loneliness lie nowhere, nowhere, but in your heart."

Dow is his own congregation, and his heart indeed contains the wild places and awesomely lonesome trails through which he endlessly rushes. His antithesis is provided by the murderous James Murrell, who suddenly rides at Dow's side, without bothering to look at him. If Dow is a mad angel, Murrell is a scarcely sane devil, talking to slow the evangelist down, without realizing that the sublimely crazy Lorenzo listens only to the voice of God:

> Murrell riding along with his victim-to-be, Murrell, riding, was Murrell talking. He told away at his long tales, with always a distance and a long length of time flowing through them, and all centered about a silent man. In each the silent man would have done a piece of evil, a robbery or a murder, in a place of long ago, and it was all made for the revelation in the end that the silent man was Murrell himself, and the long story had happened yesterday, and the place *here*—the Natchez Trace. It would only take one dawning look for the victim to see that all of this was another story and he himself had listened his way into it, and that he too was about to recede in time (to where the dread was forgotten) for some listener and to live for a listener in the long ago. Destroy the present!—that must have been the first thing that was whispered in Murrell's heart—the living moment and the man that lives in it must die before you can go on. It was his habit to bring the journey—which might even take days—to a close with a kind of ceremony. Turning his face at last into the face of the victim, for he had never seen him before now, he would tower up with the sudden height of a man no longer the tale teller but the speechless protagonist, silent at last, one degree nearer the hero. Then he would murder the man.

Since Murrell is capable of observing nothing whatsoever, he does not know what the reader knows, which is that Lorenzo is not a potential victim for this self-dramatizing Satanist. Whatever the confrontation between angel and devil might have brought (and one's surmise is that Murrell might not have survived), the crucial moment is disturbed by the arrival of a third, the even weirder Audubon:

> Audubon said nothing because he had gone without speaking a word for days. He did not regard his thoughts for the birds and animals as susceptible, in their first change, to words. His long playing on the flute was not in its origin a talking to

himself. Rather than speak to order or describe, he would always draw a deer with a stroke across it to communicate his need of venison to an Indian. He had only found words when he discovered that there is much otherwise lost that can be noted down each item in its own day, and he wrote often now in a journal, not wanting anything to be lost the way it had been, all the past, and he would write about a day, "Only sorry that the Sun Sets."

These three extraordinarily diverse obsessives share a still moment, in which "a solitary snowy heron flew down not far away and began to feed beside the marsh water." To Lorenzo, the heron's epiphany is God's love become visible. To Murrell, it is "only whiteness ensconced in darkness," a prophecy of the slave, brigand, and outcast rebellion he hopes to lead in the Natchez country. To Audubon it is precisely what it is, a white heron he must slay if he is to be able to paint, a model that must die in order to become a model. Welty gives us no preference among these three:

> What each of them had wanted was simply *all*. To save all souls, to destroy all men, to see and record all life that filled this world—all, all—but now a single frail yearning seemed to go out of the three of them for a moment and to stretch toward this one snowy, shy bird in the marshes. It was as if three whirlwinds had drawn together at some center, to find there feeding in peace a snowy heron. Its own slow spiral of flight could take it away in its own time, but for a little it held them still, it laid quiet over them, and they stood for a moment unburdened....

To quest for *all* is to know anything but peace, and "a still moment" is only shared by these three questers in a phantasmagoria. When the moment ends with Audubon's killing of the bird, only Lorenzo's horrified reaction is of deep import or interest. Murrell is content to lie back in ambush and await travelers more innocent, who will suit his Satanic destiny as Lorenzo and Audubon could not. Audubon is also content to go on, to fulfill his vast design. But Lorenzo's epiphany has turned into a negative moment and though he will go on to gather in the multitudes, he has been darkened:

In the woods that echoed yet in his ears, Lorenzo riding
slowly looked back. The hair rose on his head and his hands
began to shake with cold, and suddenly it seemed to him that
God Himself, just now, thought of the Idea of Separateness.
For surely He had never thought of it before, when the little
white heron was flying down to feed. He could understand
God's giving Separateness first and then giving Love to
follow and heal in its wonder; but God had reversed this, and
given Love first and then Separateness, as though it did not
matter to Him which came first. Perhaps it was that God
never counted the moments of Time; Lorenzo did that,
among his tasks of love. Time did not occur to God.
Therefore—did He even know of it? How to explain Time
and Separateness back to God, Who had never thought of
them, Who could let the whole world come to grief in a
scattering moment?

This is a meditation on the verge of heresy, presumably Gnostic,
rather than on the border of unbelief. Robert Penn Warren, in a classical
early essay on "Love and Separateness in Eudora Welty" (1944), reads
the dialectic of Love and Separateness here as the perhaps Blakean
contraries of Innocence and Experience. On this reading, Welty is an
ironist of limits and of contamination, for whom knowledge destroys
love, almost as though love could survive only upon enchanted ground.
That may underestimate both Lorenzo and Welty. Pragmatically,
Lorenzo has been unchanged by the still moment of love and its
shattering into separateness; indeed he is as unchanged as Murrell or
Audubon. But only Lorenzo remains haunted by a vision, by a particular
beauty greater than he can account for, and yet never can deny. He will
change some day, though Welty does not pursue that change.

II

The truth of Welty's fictive cosmos, for all her preternatural gentleness,
is that love always does come first, and always does yield to an
irreparable separateness. Like her true mentor, Twain, she triumphs in
comedy because her deepest awareness is of a nihilistic "unground"
beyond consciousness or metaphysics, and comedy is the only graceful
defense against that cosmological emptiness. Unlike Faulkner and

Flannery O'Connor, she is, by design, a genial writer, but the design is a subtler version of Twain's more urgent desperation. "A Still Moment," despite its implications, remains a fantasy of the continuities of quest. Rather than discuss one of her many masterpieces of humorous storytelling, I choose instead "The Burning," which flamboyantly displays her gift for a certain grim sublimity, and which represents her upon her heights, as a stylist and narrator who can rival Hemingway in representing the discontinuities of war and disaster.

"The Burning" belongs to the dark genre of Southern Gothic, akin to Faulkner's "A Rose for Emily" and O'Connor's "A Good Man Is Hard to Find." Welty, as historical a storyteller as Robert Penn Warren, imagines an incident from Sherman's destructive march through Georgia. The imagining is almost irrealistic in its complexity of tone and indirect representation, so that "The Burning" is perhaps the most formidable of all Welty's stories, with the kind of rhetorical and allusive difficulties we expect to encounter more frequently in modern poetry than in modern short stories. Writing on form in D.H. Lawrence's stories, Welty remarked on "the unmitigated shapelessness of Lawrence's narrative" and sharply noted that his characters would only appear deranged if they began to speak on the streets as they do in the stories:

> For the truth seems to be that Lawrence's characters don't really speak their words—not conversationally, not to one another—they are not speaking on the street, but are playing like fountains or radiating like the moon or storming like the sea, or their silence is the silence of wicked rocks. It is borne home to us that Lawrence is writing of our human relationships on earth in terms of eternity, and these terms set Lawrence's form. The author himself appears in authorship in places like the moon, and sometimes smites us while we stand there under him.

The characters of Welty's "The Burning" fit her description of Lawrence's men and women; their silence too is the silence of wicked rocks. Essentially they are only three: two mad sisters, Miss Theo and Miss Myra, and their slave, called Florabel in the story's first published version (*Harper's Bazaar*, March, 1951). The two demented high-born ladies are very different; Miss Theo is deep-voiced and domineering,

Miss Myra gentler and dependent. But little of the story is seen through their eyes or refracted through either's consciousness. Florabel, an immensely passive being, sees and reacts, in a mode not summarized until nearly the end of the story, in its first printed form:

> Florabel, with no last name, was a slave. By the time of that moment on the hill, her kind had been slaves in a dozen countries and that of their origin for thousands of years. She let everything be itself according to its nature—the animate, the inanimate, the symbol. She did not move to alter any of it, not unless she was told to and shown how. And so she saw what happened, the creation and the destruction. She waited on either one and served it, not expecting anything of it but what she got; only sooner or later she would seek protection somewhere. Herself was an unknown, like a queen, somebody she had heard called, even cried for. As a slave she was earth's most detached visitor. The world had not touched her—only possessed and hurt her, like a man; taken away from her, like a man; turned another way from her and left her, like a man. Her vision was clear. She saw what was there and had not sought it, did not seek it yet. (It was *her* eyes that were in the back of her head, her vision that met itself coming the long way back, unimpeded, like the light of stars.) The command to loot was one more fading memory. Many commands had been given her, some even held over from before she was born; delayed and miscarried and interrupted, they could yet be fulfilled, though it was safer for one once a slave to hear things a second time, a third, fourth, hundredth, thousandth, if they were to be carried out to the letter. In that noon quiet after conflict there might have been only the two triumphant, the mirror which was a symbol in the world and Florabel who was standing there; it was the rest that had died of it.

The mirror, "a symbol in the world," is in this first version of "The Burning" a synecdoche for the fragmented vision of both mad sisters and their slave. In rewriting the story, Welty uses the mirror more subtly. Delilah (as Florabel is now named) sees Sherman's soldiers and their apocalyptic white horse directly as they enter the house, and she runs to tell Miss Theo and Miss Myra. They deign to look up and observe the intruders in the mirror over the fireplace. Throughout the rest of the catastrophic narrative, the sisters behold everything that transpires as though in a mirror. Clearly they have spent their lives estranging reality as though looking in a mirror, and they move to their self-destruction as though they saw themselves only as images. The violence that prepares for the burning is thus rendered as phantasmagoria:

> The sisters showed no surprise to see soldiers and Negroes alike (old Ophelia in the way, talking, talking) strike into and out of the doors of the house, the front now the same as the back, to carry off beds, tables, candlesticks, washstands, cedar buckets, china pitchers, with their backs bent double; or the horses ready to go; or the food of the kitchen bolted down— and so much of it thrown away, this must be a second dinner; or the unsilenceable dogs, the old pack mixed with the strangers and fighting with all their hearts over bones. The last skinny sacks were thrown on the wagons—the last flour, the last scraping and clearing from Ophelia's shelves, even her pepper-grinder. The silver Delilah could count was counted on strange blankets and then, knocking against the teapot, rolled together, tied up like a bag of bones. A drummer boy with his drum around his neck caught both Miss Theo's peacocks, Marco and Polo, and wrung their necks in the yard. Nobody could look at those bird-corpses; nobody did.

The strangling of the peacocks is a presage of the weirdest sequence in "The Burning," in which Miss Theo and Miss Myra hang themselves from a tree, with Delilah assisting as ordered. It is only when the sisters are dead that we begin to understand that "The Burning" is more Delilah's story than it ever could have been theirs. A baby, Phinny, who had been allowed to perish in the fire (Welty does not allow us to know why), turns out to have been begotten by Miss Theo's and Miss Myra's brother Benton upon Delilah:

> The mirror's cloudy bottom sent up minnows of light to the brim where now a face pure as a water-lily shadow was floating. Almost too small and deep down to see, they were

quivering, leaping to life, fighting, aping old things Delilah had seen done in this world already, sometimes what men had done to Miss Theo and Miss Myra and the peacocks and to slaves, and sometimes what a slave had done and what anybody now could do to anybody. Under the flicker of the sun's licks, then under its whole blow and blare, like an unheard scream, like an act of mercy gone, as the wall-less light and July blaze struck through from the opened sky, the mirror felled her flat.

She put her arms over her head and waited, for they would all be coming again, gathering under her and above her, bees saddled like horses out of the air, butterflies harnessed to one another, bats with masks on, birds together, all with their weapons bared. She listened for the blows, and dreaded that whole army of wings—of flies, birds, serpents, their glowing enemy faces and bright kings' dresses, that banner of colors forked out, all this world that was flying, striking, stricken, falling, gilded or blackened, mortally splitting and falling apart, proud turbans unwinding, turning like the spotted dying leaves of fall, spiraling down to bottomless ash; she dreaded the fury of all the butterflies and dragonflies in the world riding, blades unconcealed and at point—descending, and rising again from the waters below, down under, one whale made of his own grave, opening his mouth to swallow Jonah one more time.

Jonah!—a homely face to her, that could still look back from the red lane he'd gone down, even if it was too late to speak. He was her Jonah, her Phinny, her black monkey; she worshiped him still, though it was long ago he was taken from her the first time.

Delilah, hysterical with fear, shock, and anguish, has fallen into the mirror world of the mad sisters, her self-slain mistresses. She is restored to some sense of reality by her search for Phinny's bones. Carrying them, and what she can save of the sisters' finery, she marches on to what is presented ambiguously either as her own freedom, or her death, or perhaps both together:

Following the smell of horses and fire, to men, she kept in the wheel tracks till they broke down at the river. In the shade underneath the burned and fallen bridge she sat on a stump and chewed for a while, without dreams, the comb of a dirtdauber. Then once more kneeling, she took a drink from the Big Black, and pulled the shoes off her feet and waded in.

Submerged to the waist, to the breast, stretching her throat like a sunflower stalk above the river's opaque skin, she kept on, her treasure stacked on the roof of her head, hands laced upon it. She had forgotten how or when she knew, and she did not know what day this was, but she knew—it would not rain, the river would not rise, until Saturday.

This extraordinary prose rises to an American sublime that is neither grotesque nor ironic. Welty, in her *On Short Stories*, asked the question: "Where does beauty come from, in the short story?" and answered only that beauty was a result:

It *comes*. We are lucky when beauty comes, for often we try and it should come, it could, we think, but then when the virtues of our story are counted, beauty is standing behind the door.

I do not propose to count the virtues of "The Burning," or even of "A Still Moment." Both narratives are as thoroughly written through, fully composed, as the best poems of Wallace Stevens or of Hart Crane, or the strongest of Hemingway's stories, or Faulkner's *As I Lay Dying*. American writing in the twentieth century touches the sublime mode only in scattered instances, and always by reaching the frontier where the phantasmagoric, and the realism of violence, are separated only by ghostlier demarcations, keener sounds. Welty's high distinction is that in her the demarcations are as ghostly, the sounds as keen, as they are in her greatest narrative contemporaries, Faulkner and Hemingway.

AMY SICKELS

Biography of Eudora Welty

SHELTERED BEGINNINGS

"I am a writer who came out of a sheltered life. A sheltered life can be a daring life as well. For all serious daring starts within," states Eudora Welty in her memoir, *One Writer's Beginnings* (114).

Eudora Welty was born and raised in Jackson, Mississippi; she came of age in the Deep South during a time of extreme segregation and rigid social mores. As a white, upper-middle class woman she was delegated to a certain "place" in society, in which she was protected and nurtured by her hometown and her parents. For her childhood and adolescence, she lived happily within this constructed nest.

Welty would be nudged from this nest and her eyes opened during the Depression Era when she went to work for the Works Progress Administration (WPA). For her job she traveled all around Mississippi, admitting, "I saw my home state at close hand, really for the first time" (*OWB* 92). Whatever she saw, she recorded with her camera. Welty took hundreds of black and white photographs, mostly of African-Americans, capturing their daily actions in a land of extreme poverty and prejudice. It was here, in the rural, depressed areas of Mississippi, and away from her comfortable home on Pinehurst Street, that Welty discovered the kernels for her first stories. She observed everything around her with acuteness and compassion; both her photographs and stories revealed her emphasis on specificity, place, and her lifetime subject, human relationships. Photography and fiction overlapped in their demand for

Welty to pay attention to the human condition—to notice the losses and hardships, as well as the humor and resilience.

Although it was fiction that she would finally devote herself to, photography influenced her creativity and her way of seeing. Welty called herself a "visual writer," and she often spoke about the importance of place in fiction. Most of her stories were set in Mississippi, the place which she knew best. Although Welty traveled widely, she always returned to her hometown, where she lived her entire life.

Welty's fiction tends to focus on the microscopic and domestic; she does not write novels that take place in great socio-political arenas, and often she was criticized for this style of writing. However, for Welty—who paid such close attention to the subtle and particular details of the human condition—personal, intimate relationships were far more powerful and revealing than political agendas.

Welty often described the writing life as something that happened in the interior, and she made a clear distinction between interior/exterior and privacy/public in her famous essay, "Must the Novelist Crusade?":

> Writing fiction is an interior affair. Novels and stories always will be put down little by little out of personal feeling and personal beliefs arrived at alone and at firsthand over a period of time as time is needed. To go outside and beat the drum is only to interrupt, interrupt, and so finally to forget and to lose. Fiction has, and must keep, a private address. For life is *lived* in a private place; where it means anything is inside the mind and heart. (*Eudora Welty: Stories, Essays & Memoir* 809)

Welty's emphasis on privacy very much included her own life. She refused to talk about personal matters and would never agree to a biography; when one was written about her, she actively tried to stop its publication.

Yet, these lines between the private/personal, or the interior/exterior often blurred in Welty's fiction and in her own life. Although she may have eschewed politics from her fiction, because she was writing about the complexity of human relationships, her fiction often reveals social concerns, including racism and sexism. Furthermore, although Welty spoke of her sheltered life and privacy, she did not hide from the public eye. She gave hundreds of interviews, and lived a socially-rich life. She was friends with people from several different literary circles, including Robert Penn Warren, Katherine Anne Porter, Elizabeth Bowen, V.S. Pritchett, Shelby Foote, Walker Percy, Elizabeth Spencer, Allen Tate, Ross McDonald, and Reynolds Price. Her friends were very important to her, as were her travels to Europe and New York City. She may have always returned to Jackson, but she also recognized the importance of leaving.

Welty's close observations of the world around her, from the humorous dialogue to the socio-economic particulars of a region, appeared in all of her fiction. Yet it was also her rich, daring imagination which led to the creation of her most memorable characters. Observation and imagination, or the exterior and the interior, connected and overlapped in Welty's stories and novels. It was also Welty's faith in humanity that brought her fiction to life: "And so finally I think we need to write with love. Not in self-defense, not in hate, not in the mood of instruction, not in rebuttal, in any kind of militance, or in apology, but with love" (*Stories, Essays & Memoir* 812).

JACKSON, MISSISSIPPI

Eudora Alice Welty was born on April 13, 1909 to Christian and Chestina Welty in Jackson, Mississippi. Her parents were not originally from the Deep South, a detail which set the family slightly apart from most of the other Jackson citizens. Her father, an only child of a farmer of German-Swiss ancestry, grew up in rural Ohio. Her mother hailed from the mountains of West Virginia where she lived with her widowed mother and five brothers. Although Christian and Chestina grew up in very different types of families, both of them had experienced the early death of a parent. Christian's mother died when he was seven years old; Chestina's father, a country lawyer and farmer, died when she was fifteen.

Christian Webb Welty met Chestina, a school teacher, when he was working for a lumber mill in West Virginia. Christian strongly believed in "progress" and the promises of the future, and he wanted to leave the impoverished area and move to a growing town. He investigated and researched different areas of the United States, and then asked his fiancée if she would rather live in the Finger Lakes region of New York or in Jackson, Mississippi. She chose the south. They were married on October 13, 1904, and shortly after, packed up and moved to the capital of Mississippi. In those days it was quite unusual for a couple to leave their ancestral home and move to an entirely different part of the country. But Chestina and Christian were young and eager to start a family in a place that was new to them.

Christian had been right about the growth of Jackson. When the Weltys arrived, the population was in the process of doubling to twenty thousand in 1910. Christian worked for Lamar Life Insurance Company; over the years he climbed the ranks until he eventually rose to the position of president. He was in charge of many important projects, including the design and construction of the company headquarters, a thirteen story "skyscraper" in downtown Jackson across from the governor's residence. For his family, he built a two and a half story house on North Congress Street, near the new capital building, where Welty and her younger brothers were born. Her brother Edward was born three years after Welty, and Walter followed in 1915.

By all accounts, Welty had a happy, quiet childhood. She lovingly described her parents as devoted and protective, a combination which influenced her introspective and friendly personality. Part of their protectiveness may have stemmed from an earlier tragedy—their first child, a boy, died at birth, which was something they did not discuss. Welty spent her early childhood days playing typical games with her brothers, such as jacks and hopscotch. She and Edward shared a love for humor and silliness, and liked to make each other laugh. According to Welty, she also sometimes threw temper tantrums, hitting objects or slamming doors: "I was responsible for scenes" (*OWB* 42).

Although protective, Chestina and Christian also encouraged independence and discovery, and, in different ways, both influenced Welty's chosen path as a writer. Her father's unwavering belief in progress had brought the family to Jackson, and his fascination with machines, such as telescopes and cameras, affected Welty's own interest in time, travel, and photography. Her mother's influence was more obvious and direct: Chestina loved to read. She once raced into a burning house to rescue a full set of Dickens, a present from her father. She read extensively and deeply, including *Jane Eyre*, Robert Louis Stevenson, the Bible, and Charles Darwin. Welty always knew there was a good chance she would find her mother reading, in any room of the house at any time of the day.

Reading was an integral part of Welty's childhood and she was drawn to books the way other children love sweets: "I cannot remember a time when I was not in love with them—with the books themselves, cover and binding and the paper they were printed on, with their smell and their weight and with their possession in my arms, captured and carried off to myself" (*OWB* 6). She learned to read at a young age, her mother enrolling her in the first grade at five years old, and she devoured everything she could get her hands on: Grimm's fairy tales, Greek and Roman mythology, legends, series books, encyclopedias, and many popular and literary titles. Once, when she was seven, she was taken out of school for a "fast-beating heart" and she spent a few months confined to bed, reading ravenously. Although she hated not being in school, she admitted that the enforced rest gave her "a glorious opportunity to do what I loved to do: Read" (*More Conversations* 168). At nine years old, she began to visit the local Andrew Carnegie Library, where she checked out two books a day. The two-book limit was imposed by the strict librarian, Mrs. Calloway, who also sent girls home if she could see through their skirts; Welty wore two petticoats, just to be safe.

Growing up in Jackson shaped Welty's style as a fiction writer on several levels. The most obvious influence was setting, as most of her stories take place in Mississippi. In addition, the Southern culture of storytelling and the flavor of local speech contributed to Welty's sharp ear for writing dialogue. Not only did she read extensively, Welty also listened closely: "Long before I wrote stories, I listened for stories" (*OWB* 16). She loved to hear all types of stories, whether true, or gossip, or folktales.

However, because her parents were not originally from Mississippi (and her father was a Yankee) many of her experiences differed from those of her childhood friends. For example, many of the Jackson families had been there for several generations, and they told personal stories of the Civil War, such as how the old family house was burned. Welty did not have strong ties to Southern history in this way, and her parents provided her with different perspectives. "It was a good family to grow up in," she explained. "I learned there wasn't just one side that was right" (*Conversations* 33).

Religion was also important to the South. Although Welty attended Sunday school and her mother often read the Bible, her

Methodist family "was never a churchgoing family" (*OWB* 34), another detail which set them apart from tradition. Still, the religious influence of the town permeated into Welty's upbringing, and she once cited the King James Version of the Bible as an indirect influence on her own writing as well as on most southern writers: "Its cadence entered into our ears and our memories for good" (37).

Even as a young child, Welty looked forward to seeing other places. The only time she left Jackson was to visit her grandparents in Ohio and West Virginia. The mountains of West Virginia especially impressed her, and she recognized her mother's attachment. Welty believed that her mother had never completely adjusted to Mississippi: "I think she could listen sometimes and hear the mountain's voice" (*OWB* 59). While her father looked to the future, her mother held onto the past, enchanted by family stories and legends, and both views informed Welty's sensibilities.

As Welty grew older, she never lost her joy for literature. In high school the subjects she most enjoyed were literature and art. She wrote for the school newspaper and was the art editor for the yearbook. She performed well in all subjects, although whenever she did not receive a 100% on a test, her mother "took it personally" (*OWB* 27). Chestina strove for excellence, and Welty casually explained, "It was unclouded perfection I was up against" (27).

Welty socialized widely, but she did not date or attend dances. Her closest friends were a group of intelligent, funny, and literary boys who also wanted to be writers. They would be her friends for life. The unauthorized biographer Ann Waldron interviewed several of Welty's former classmates, who admitted that Welty was a not a traditional Southern belle. They described her as quite tall, and said she always stood with her shoulders hunched, as if trying to hide her height. However, she was popular, named "Best All Round Girl," and people were drawn to her kind and humorous personality (Waldron 10). "The pity for Eudora Welty was that she was not pretty, that she was tall, and that her parents were not from the South," suggests Waldron. "The blessing was that she was smart, that she was very nice, and that her father was a prominent, well-liked citizen in town" (11).

It was during Welty's high school years that her father built a new house for the family on Pinehurst Street. The street was then a gravel road, with several pines and an oak tree residing on the property. The house, a six-room 1920's dark red brick Tudor house, resembled Northern architecture instead of Southern. This would be the house where Welty would live for the rest of her life.

Like her family home, Jackson itself was safe, protective, and supportive. Life in Jackson, from childhood to high school graduation, later filled Welty with warm nostalgia. Although Jackson's population doubled during the 1920s and continued to grow steadily, it was certainly not a bustling big city. Welty described her childhood as consisting of "small-town, unhurried days" (*OWB* 40). Jackson was a sleepy, untroubled place in which to grow up.

Nearly half of Jackson's population, however, did not live in this idealistic setting. Jackson was a highly segregated society, and African Americans were pushed out to the impoverished, neglected areas of the city. Whites did not intermingle with blacks, except in employer-servant relationships. In fact, one of Welty's contemporaries, whom she never met, was Richard Wright, the author of *Native Son*. He also lived in Jackson, attending the all-black high school. "Nothing could illuminate the horror and stupidity of the segregated South more vividly than the fact that Richard Wright and Eudora Welty never met, although they were the same age, had similar interests, and lived in the same town for several years," asserts biographer Ann Waldron. "The picture that Eudora paints in her memoir of Jackson as a safe, comfortable town where families walked in the park for band concerts on summer evenings becomes a mockery when it is compared with Wright's hand-to-mouth existence in the rundown, poorly lit, unsanitary black section of town" (16). Welty, sheltered by her surroundings, did not seem to even be aware of the juxtaposition between the quality of life for whites and blacks; as a child and adolescent, she had no interactions with African Americans. When an interviewer once asked if she overheard stories from black people when she was growing up, she replied, "Not from black people, mostly because I never saw black people then except in a white household as a servant or something, and though I would hear bits of superstition or remarks that I later remember, I never heard black people talking among themselves. I heard many white people" (*More Conversations* 14). Welty's experience was not unusual during this time, and it would not be for several more years that Mississippi would be forced to acknowledge and deal with its institutionalized racism.

"Passion" for Literature

Welty graduated from Central High School in 1925; she was only sixteen years old. She wanted to go to college out of state, but her parents thought she was too young. Instead, they allowed her to attend the Mississippi State College for Women in Columbus, 150 miles northeast of Jackson. MSCW, founded in 1884, was a state school; however, at that time, it was steeped in Christian-based codes. Students were required to attend chapel twice a week and to wear uniforms with skirts no shorter than ten inches from the floor. Playing bridge was forbidden, and after the night whistle blew, the campus gates were locked. Yet for Welty, who had never been away from Jackson except to visit her grandparents, college provided an exciting opportunity to be away from home and to meet new people.

The 1,200 girls came from all over Mississippi, representing nearly every region of the state, from the Delta to the Gulf Coast. Welty was fascinated by the different dialects and habits: "This was my first chance to learn what the body of us were like and what differences in background, persuasion of mind, and resources of character there were among Mississippians—at that, among only half of us, for we were all white" (*OWB* 84). Many of the girls were quite poor, and the school itself had very little money. However, college provided Welty with a wealth of writing and artistic experiences.

Welty participated in many extracurricular activities. She wrote skits and plays, and performed in most of the productions. She also took photographs for the yearbook; provided cartoons and poems for the school paper, *The Spectator;* and helped to create the humor magazine, *Oh, Lady!* until the president of the college shut it down. She took classes in Latin, French, English, history, and art, and wrote melodramatic short stories about Paris, one which opened with the line: "Monsieur Boule deposited a delicate dagger in Mademoiselle's left side and departed with a poised immediacy" (*Conversations* 3). She was popular and well-liked, and entertained the students with her cartoons and plays. Once, to the other girls' delight, she wrote to the chairman of the Hershey company and told him the students at MSCW were starving, and soon after, a case of Hershey bars arrived (Waldron 32).

After two years (1925–27) her parents decided she was old enough to go out of state, and Welty transferred to the University of Wisconsin, a progressive, well-respected college with a strong intellectual atmosphere. She majored in English and minored in art history. In high school she had flirted with the idea of being an artist, but she discovered the limits to her artistic ability when she enrolled in an art class at Wisconsin. "I felt the shock ... when I walked into my art class and saw, in place of the bowl of fruit and the glass bottle and ginger jar of the still life I used to draw at MSCW, a live human being" who "dropped her robe" (*OWB* 87). Her art teacher suggested Welty go to the library and practice drawing statues because she did not know enough about anatomy to draw the human figure.

English classes introduced her to a wide range of literature. She read Proust, Mann, and Chekhov. She became a fan of Irish writers, especially of W.B. Yeats. The diverse readings inspired her, particularly a class on 18th century literature, in which the teacher, Ricardo Quintana, used the word "passion" to describe literature: "I had never heard a teacher use the word 'passion' before, and it really taught me what was meant by that word, and the whole meaning of the poetic imagination" (*More Conversations* 5).

Although her academic education at Wisconsin was fulfilling, she did not have a robust social life the way she had at MSCW. Welty did not participate in the drama clubs nor did she connect with other writers. "It is hard to account for this invisibility when Eudora had been so active and popular at MSCW," acknowledges Waldron. "Contributing factors were undoubtedly the fact that she was a transfer student, her shyness in the strange environment, and her southernness" (39). Waldron suspects that Welty was depressed during these years, homesick for the South. Her housemates described her as shy, yet smart and charming, and "a lovely girl, but so plain" (Waldron 37). Welty helped the girls get ready to go on dates, but did not go on any herself.

A FATHER'S SUPPORT

Living in Jackson informed and shaped Eudora Welty's sense of place and her devotion to friends and family, but she also yearned for new experiences. She graduated with her B.A. in 1929, and by the summer, she knew she wanted to be a writer. She applied to several publishing houses in New York City. Her father was worried that she would not be able to make a living as a writer. He was also wary of fiction, although Welty claimed he did show support: "He said, it's not the truth about life. And he thought I might be wasting my life ... But he did support me" (*More Conversations* 147).

Welty enrolled in Columbia University's School of Business to study advertising, a move that pleased her father and gave her the opportunity to leave the South. In the fall of 1930 she arrived in New York with three other Jackson girls. Several of her friends were also in New York at the time, including Frank Lyell, Lehman Engel, and Herschell Brickell—a former editor of the *Jackson Daily News* who would become an important figure in the New York literary world. Welty soaked in the sights and sounds of the city. She attended theater, museums, and galleries. She spent time in Greenwich Village and went to night clubs in Harlem.

Then, in the fall of 1931, when she was twenty-two years old, she received news that her beloved father was dying of leukemia, and she quickly returned to Mississippi. In a last effort to save his life, the doctor tried a blood transfusion; however, doctors at that time did not fully understand that unless blood types were exactly matched, the procedure could be lethal. Welty's mother agreed to give blood, and during the transfusion, Christian died. "My mother never recovered emotionally," Welty later wrote. "Though she lived for over thirty years more, and suffered other bitter losses, she never stopped blaming herself. She saw this as her failure to save his life" (*OWB* 101). Welty's father died on September 23, 1931. He was fifty-two years old. Welty, in her grief, must have been just as emotionally distraught as her mother. Many years later Welty recalled, "What I remember is that there were venetian blinds in back of me, that the heat of the sun was coming through the slats and onto my back. I suppose that was my creeping horror. That's what a person remembers—the physical sensation. I'd never seen anyone die before" (*More Conversations* 80).

LOCAL LITERARY CIRCLE

Welty decided to stay in Jackson with her mother (her brothers were away at college). Her father's investments and insurance temporarily relieved the family of financial problems, but Welty still held a variety of jobs for the next few years. For her first job she was a copywriter for WJDX, Jackson's first radio station, that was housed in the building her father founded. Her next job was writing the society pages for the Mississippi newspaper the *Memphis Commercial Appeal*. At one point she traveled to New York for six weeks to look for work, but she was unsuccessful and returned again to Jackson.

She held these jobs during the period of the Great Depression, which Welty claimed did not affect Mississippi as much as it did the rest of the country because Mississippi was already so incredibly poor. She spent these years socializing with a close group of accomplished, ambitious friends that included Hubert Creekmore, Nash Burger, Frank Lyell, Lehman Engel, Bill Hamilton, and John Robinson. Creekmore and Burger, high school classmates, both wrote fiction. Creekmore tirelessly sent out his work to magazines, and was an early influence on Welty; Nash Burger taught English at Central High. Lyell, earning his Ph.D. at Princeton, taught at North Carolina State and then the University of Texas, and returned to Jackson every summer. Engel had been to Julliard, and later became a top Broadway composer and conductor. Hamilton, teaching history at Central High, later went on to write books and edit the *South Atlantic Quarterly*. His fraternity brother John Robinson, an ongoing student, joined the crowd and became close friends with Welty.

The twenty-some-year-olds managed to entertain themselves during those lean years. They spent evenings listening to jazz records and sometimes drinking bourbon. Because of Prohibition, whenever they wanted to drink, they had to cross Pearl River over into Rankin County. The bootlegger was always moving the location of his business to evade the law. Once Welty encountered a young black boy, reading *Time* magazine, and, without lifting his eyes from the page, he silently raised his arm to point her to the new location. Years later, Welty recalled:

> Now that I think back on those days, I know they must have been very bad times indeed, but actually, I'm not sure we realized it, my friends and I. We were all so naïve, so inexperienced, right out of school. We sort of found our own ways of having fun. We invented methods of entertainment, things that didn't cost anything. You could go on a picnic, a dozen people, for practically nothing. (*Conversations* 145)

The group had a witty sense of humor and loved any sort of excitement. They played charades and word games, and sometimes threw little dinner parties, dressing up in costumes like the people in *Vanity Fair*. They were interested in art, literature, and culture; they all faithfully read *The New Yorker*. Sometimes they took road trips to Alabama or New Orleans, where they listened to jazz. "It was very easy to go down there and get into this completely different world," Welty said (*More Conversations* 252). The group of friends would take a train to spend the day in the French Quarter, none of them having enough money to stay overnight. Once Welty and her friends saw the blues singer Bessie Smith perform at the Alamo, a black movie house. They knew the owner, and were able to get seats. As they were the only white patrons, they sat in the balcony: "Just where we made black people sit in those days when they came to our movie houses," she acknowledged. "We were glad to be allowed in; it was a real, real compliment" (*More Conversations* 128). Social time was extremely important for Welty and her friends. Young and hopeful, they were filled with passion for art and literature, and their social circle remained close throughout their lives.

PHOTOGRAPHY

In 1935 Welty went to work in the publicity department for the Works Progress Administration (WPA), one of President Franklin Roosevelt's programs to create jobs during the Depression. As a junior publicity agent, she promoted and publicized WPA projects, such as road building, new airstrips, or canning factories. This job gave her the opportunity to travel all over Mississippi; she visited nearly every single one of the eighty-two counties in the state. It was an education which neither college nor New York City had provided: she observed the geographical diversity of her state, but also the dire poverty of the different regions. She was fascinated and troubled by what she saw.

These travels stimulated Welty to record what she witnessed through stories and photographs. She took hundreds of snapshots with a cheap camera, and developed the prints at home in the kitchen. She started out with a small Eastman Kodak which used number 116 film, and later moved on to a Rolliflex. Although she was not an official WPA photographer, the organization did publish some of her photographs. Welty photographed extensively, taking pictures of political rallies, revival meetings, and the daily actions of the people of the towns. She photographed young and old, blacks and whites; most of the hundreds of pictures were of African Americans. Waldron remarks on how unusual this was: "To upper-class white women like Eudora, black people were then virtually invisible, except when they were servants. Her independent perception of them as worthy of her time and attention in the 1930s is one of the most astonishing and admirable facets of Eudora Welty's character" (Waldron 74). Welty had spent her entire childhood and adolescence without any contact with African Americans; now she clearly saw how the "other" Mississippi citizens lived.

She always first politely asked her subjects for permission to photograph them, and, according to Welty, they always said yes. She did not worry about "proper" boundaries between blacks and whites: she simply recorded what she saw: "They weren't special pictures, but pictures of life as it was" (*Conversations* 146). Nobody ever protested: "If I saw something happening that I wanted to take a picture of, I'd just go up and tell the person to keep on doing what he was doing while I took a picture. And they always did! You couldn't do that today, you know" (*Conversations* 151). The experience taught her about human relationships and interaction with each other, as she recognized that she was "coming upon people I didn't know and taking this minute of their lives" (*Conversations* 151).

Photography taught her about the powers of observation and perspective, and also "helped her to understand that Mississippi was worth writing about" (Waldron 76). Several of Welty's stories emerged from what she saw and heard as she traveled around the state. For example, she once saw an ironing board in a county post office, and the image bloomed into one of her most beloved stories, "Why I Live at the P.O." Another time she overheard a story about a black man in a carnival, forced to eat live chickens, and she wrote "Keela, the Outcast Indian Maid." Not only did she find ideas for her stories, but the act of photography also influenced the techniques of her fiction:

> I learned in the doing how *ready* I had to be. Life doesn't hold still.... Photography taught me that to be able to capture transience, by being ready to click the shutter at the crucial moment, was the greatest need I had. Making pictures of people in all sorts of situations, I learned that every feeling waits upon its gesture; and I had to be prepared to recognize this moment when I saw it. These were things a story writer

needed to know. And I felt the need to hold transient life in *words*—there's so much more of life that only words can convey—strongly enough to last me as long as I lived. The direction my mind took was a writer's direction from the start, not a photographer's or a recorder's. (*OWB* 84)

At first Welty was satisfied in just sharing her photographs with friends, but then she began traveling to New York to show the photographs to publishers along with a set of short stories.

Although Welty's permanent residence was on Pinehurst Street, she often went on trips. She loved to travel, and was especially fond of New York City, which was like a second home. She appreciated the rich cultural life and the access to art and literature. She would take a train from Jackson to Washington, and then take a special train from Washington to New York, which then cost $3.50, round-trip.

Every time Welty left for one of her trips, she knew that her mother was waiting for her to come back: "I knew that even as I was moving farther away from Jackson, my mother was already writing to me at her desk, telling me she missed me but only wanted what was best for me" (*OWB* 102). While Chestina Welty encouraged Welty's independence, she also did not to want to let go of her daughter, a contradiction Welty addresses in her memoir: "Yet, while she knew that independent spirit so well, it was what she so agonizingly tried to protect me from, in effect to warn me against. It was what we shared, it made the strongest bond between us and the strongest tension" (66). Waldron describes Welty's relationship with her mother as "complicated and conflicted" which continued in this way until her mother's death many years later (83). Chestina was overprotective and often demanding, yet she was also devoted, generous, and proud of her daughter. Welty admitted her mother could easily make her feel guilty: "I continued to feel that bliss for me would have to imply my mother's deprivation or sacrifice" (*OWB* 21). While Welty would never abandon her mother, she did manage to take yearly trips to New York.

None of the publishers accepted her work, neither the manuscripts or the photographs, but she did get a chance to exhibit her photographs at Lugene Optics, a camera shop on Madison Avenue. The owner agreed to show her work and also gave her tips on photo development, advising her on chemicals and paper. He exhibited the show, with a statement that the photographs had been printed in Mississippi "under primitive conditions" (*More Conversations* 189). When many years later some of these photographs were collected in a book, Welty quipped that this was not a show people actually knew about: "It wasn't a gallery, it was a shop, and even if reviewers had seen the show, they would have found it enough to say that here are primitive pictures by an unknown from Mississippi" (*More Conversations* 189).

Years later, Welty's photographs would be compiled and published in two different books, and although her photographs were not as technically proficient as the famous WPA photographers Walker Evans and Dorothea Lange, her work sometimes drew comparisons. However, Welty, who never saw Evans' work until years after the WPA, did not like his "deliberately composed" photographs (*More Conversations* 197). She added, "I let my subjects go on with what they were doing and, by framing or cutting and by selection, found what composition rose from that. So, I think that's a quality that makes them different from those of professionals who were purposefully photographing for an agency, or cause" (*More Conversations* 197). Welty expressed disdain for what seemed like exploitation, and biographer Waldron concurs that "her soft-focus, low-contrast work shows a compassion for the people she photographed that is often missing in Evans's work" (Waldron 76). Similar to her photographs, Welty's fiction demonstrates her desire to portray the lives of people—and not a particular agenda.

THE EARLY STORIES AND *THE SOUTHERN REVIEW*

Welty's job with the WPA ended in 1936 with defeat of the Democratic party, and she started to devote herself more to writing fiction. She was too shy to show her work to any of her literary friends, but she did ask her writer friend Hubert Creekmore what she should do with her stories. He suggested she submit a story to *Manuscript*, a small magazine published in Ohio. Welty sent two stories, "Magic" and "Death of a Traveling Salesman," and the editor and publisher, John Rood, surprised Welty by sending her a praising letter of acceptance. "That was the first time I sent him a story, and immediately, he took it," she said. "And I thought, 'Is that they way it happens? You just put something in the mail and they say okay?' Well, I was just lucky" (*More Conversations* 292). The story is about a traveling salesman, feverish and ill, who loses his way among the back roads and stops at a cabin, where he meets a young, rural couple. This early story exemplifies Welty's skill in writing about characters outside of herself: as a single white woman, she often wrote from the perspectives of middle-aged men, as in this case, or African-Americans, or married couples. She explained, "In writing fiction, I think imagination comes ahead of sex. A writer's got to be able to live inside all characters: male, female, old, young. To live inside any other person is the jump. Whether the other persons are male or female is subordinate" (*Conversations* 54).

The publication of "Death of a Traveling Salesman" in that small magazine was the spark that set off Welty's writing career, and the story also revealed to Welty the central subject of all of her fiction: "I had received the shock of having touched, for the first time, on my real subject: human relationships" (*OWB* 95).

After this publication, many rejections followed. Undaunted, the twenty-eight year old Welty continued to write and send out her work. Then to her delight, the critic and author Robert Penn Warren, editor of the *Southern Review*, bought her short story "A Piece of News" in May 1937. Robert Penn Warren was one of the Fugitive poets, a group of Vanderbilt University writers, also including Allen Tate and John Crowe Ransom, whom Welty and her friends had been reading. This was the first money she earned for her fiction; she used the earnings to screen the front porch (which cost under $42).

Welty sent out more stories, and when she wasn't writing, she spent time doing what she loved best: socializing with her Jackson friends, listening to music, and gardening. She also took on the occasional odd job. She worked for the Mississippi Advertising commission, writing copy and taking photos to attract industry and tourism to the state. The job, however, did not detract her from writing. Although many stories were rejected, others were accepted. Warren bought two more stories, "A Memory" and "Old Mr. Grenada," and *Prairie Schooner* accepted the story "Flowers for Marjorie." Welty was writing quite frequently and turning out many stellar short stories. At this point in her career, she did not ever revise: she just wrote the stories and then sent them out. Once Warren asked for another look at her story, "The Petrified Man," which he had already rejected. Welty, in frustration of the story's many rejections, had actually burned her only copy of the manuscript. So she sat down and rewrote the story from memory. Warren published "The Petrified Man" in the spring of 1939, and it was then chosen for the O. Henry Prize Stories anthology.

Welty was fortunate enough to be praised by prominent authors and critics quite early in her career. She was now a favorite contributor to the *Southern Review*, and although she had not yet met Warren in person, the two became friends by mail. She also caught the attention of Albert Erskine, who was married to the author Katherine Anne Porter for a short time. He was on the staff of the *Southern Review* and years later would be a distinguished editor Random House. Katherine Anne Porter, the esteemed author of *Flower Judas and Other Stories, Hacienda*, and *Noon Wine*, wrote Welty a letter of praise after reading her stories in the *Southern Review*. Porter also told Ford Maddox Ford about this talented young writer. Ford, a novelist and literary critic who had published over eighty books, was in now in charge of Dial Press and apparently tried to help Welty out by contacting publishers. Welty reminisced, "As you may know, Ford spent vast energies all his life helping young people. I was one of them, probably the last of a long list. It was just a great, generous spirit he had. He wrote to me out of a blue sky and asked if he could help in any way in interesting a publisher" (*Conversations* 40). Welty was always grateful for his support; however, he died before he sent out her work.

Although she never had the chance to meet Ford, Welty received a letter from Katherine Anne Porter inviting Welty to visit her in Baton Rouge. Welty attempted the trip twice, but she was nervous, and both times only got as far as Natchez before she turned back around. Finally, in July, 1939, she made the trip with her friend Herschel Brickell and his wife Norma. The meeting between Porter and Welty was the beginning of a lasting friendship: "Katherine Anne Porter and Welty became friends, or rather generous mentor and devoted protégé, and remained friends, though sometimes uneasy ones, until Porter's death" (Waldron 96).

Welty continued to develop relationships with writers and editors, but she could not find a publisher willing to buy her story collection. Various publishers noticed her talent, but they wanted a novel, which was more salable. She even had a visit from a publisher. John Woodburn, an editor from Doubleday, went to the South scouting new writers, and heard about Eudora Welty. He stopped by her home, and she showed him her photographs, while her mother cooked waffles for him. When he left, he took Welty's short stories back to New York. He was hopeful about her work; however, he had to return the manuscript after Doubleday rejected the collection.

NATIONAL EXPOSURE

Welty continued sending out the collection to publishers and submitting new stories to magazines. Then in May 1940, Welty received a letter "out of a clear blue sky" from a literary agent named Diarmuid Russell (*Conversations* 41). Russell was the son of George William Russell, known as A.E., the Irish writer whose work Welty had read at Wisconsin. Diarmuid had been an editor at Putnam before he started his own agency; it was the editor at Doubleday, John Woodburn, who suggested Welty as a possible client. Welty didn't even know what a literary agent was, but she wrote him back, saying, yes, "Be my agent!" He wrote back, "Wait! You don't know a thing about me. I may be a crook!" (*More Conversations* 218)

This was the start of a long and devoted relationship between Welty and Diarmuid; he would remain her agent until his death in 1973. Welty quickly sent him her newest stories, and he was impressed by the breadth and scope of her writing. He submitted her story collection to publisher after publisher, and it continued to be rejected. Editors, such as the famed Maxwell Perkins at Scribner's, recognized Welty as a talented writer, but didn't want to gamble on publishing a first collection. Even with the slew of rejections, Welty and Diarmuid's faith in each other—as writer and agent—never wavered. Russell was devoted to and supportive of her writing, reading and commenting on every manuscript she sent to him, and Welty, throughout her career, often went to him when faced with publisher's questions or criticisms.

When she was thirty-one years old, Welty attended the Bread Loaf writer's conference, after Katherine Anne Porter had recommended her for a fellowship. Bread Loaf was part of Middlebury College in Vermont, and the summer writing conference was the first of its kind in the country. The eight fellows received free tuition, room and board, and attended workshops and listened to speakers. Although the conference was a good way to make literary contacts, Welty did not enjoy her time there. She did not find the workshops to be at all helpful. For example, one workshop unanimously decided that Welty's story "Powerhouse" would never be published. She had written the story, about a black jazz musician on the road, after attending a Fats Waller concert in Jackson—she had come home that night and written the story in one sitting. When an interviewer asked how she knew to write in the lingo of black jazz musicians, she explained, "Oh, I was listening to them. I was one of those people who were just hanging around listening.... I had no idea I was going to write anything when I went to that. I would've thought, rightly, 'You don't know anything.' It's true, I didn't. But I was so excited by the evening that I wrote it, after I got home. And the next day when I woke up I said, 'How could I have had the nerve to do something like that?'(*Conversations* 327).

According to Waldron, Welty also had an unpleasant time at the conference because she had an extreme dislike for one of the other fellows, a young southern writer named Carson McCullers. McCullers, author of *The Heart is the Lonely Hunter, Reflections in a Golden Eye,* and *The Ballad of the Sad Café,* had a reputation for being flamboyant, and a drinker. Welty "detested Carson McCullers for her pretensions and poses" (Waldron 103). However, years later when an interviewer asked about McCullers, Welty, always gracious, only said, "We were up there for a week at the same time. We never were intimate, and it never came about that we were later" (*More Conversations* 61). Welty spent most of her time at Bread Loaf with Katherine Anne Porter, who was one of the lecturers. Welty admired Porter for her success as a writer. She was beautiful and commanding, and she enjoyed spending time with the young Welty, describing her as "a quiet, tranquil-looking, modest girl" ("Introduction" 151). The writer Wallace Stegner observed them at Bread Loaf: "Porter enthroned in an armchair, holding forth in her soft Texas accent, with Eudora sitting worshipfully at her feet" (Waldron 104).

On her return to Jackson, Welty began to think about a new book. She was greatly interested in Mississippi history, and particularly in the Old Natchez Trace, which had been important highway in the old southwest. It was 450 miles long and connected Nashville to Natchez, and was once used by Indians, outlaws, evangelists, and settlers. Her interest and curiosity turned into the form of a long tale called *The Robber Bridegroom,* her most fantastical and mythical piece. She finished the manuscript and sent it to Russell, and although he liked the tale, he knew he would have trouble selling it. Woodburn admired the story, but didn't accept it for publication, and he suggested Welty write a whole book of stories about this particular area of Mississippi, something Welty took to heart.

Welty's work continued to be rejected, but she had a great deal of support from Russell, Porter, Woodburn, and all of her Jackson friends, such as Nash Burger and John Robinson. Then, in an astonishing surprise, on December 3, 1940, Russell sold two of her stories to Edward A. Weeks at the *Atlantic Monthly*. After six years of sending out stories, Welty was finally published in a national magazine. She was always grateful to Russell for this breakthrough: "If it hadn't been for him, I don't know if I'd have ever been published. I really mean it, because he worked like everything just because he believed in my stories" (*More Conversations* 22).

Weeks published "A Worn Path," now one of Welty's most anthologized stories, in which Phoenix Jackson, an old black woman, walks along the Old Natchez Trace to the clinic in town to get medicine for her grandson. The other story Weeks bought was "Powerhouse." Although she was disappointed that the *Atlantic Monthly* chose to censor the lyrics to "Hold Tight, I Want Some Seafood Mama," the song Welty had chosen to use for its vivid line, "fooly racky sacky, want some seafood, Mama," she nonetheless was honored and delighted with the publication. Weeks paid her $200 for each story, and then in February he bought a third story, "Why I Live at the P.O.," another one of Welty's most popular stories that illustrates her sense of humor. With the money from the *Atlantic*, Welty bought a Fats Waller record, flower and vegetable seeds, and a telescope from Sears, Roebuck.

WRITER AT WORK

With this national exposure, Welty attracted more attention. Soon after the *Atlantic's* purchase of her stories, Woodburn asked for another look at her story collection. This time Doubleday bought the collection.

During the time of the collection's acceptance and its publication date, Welty was busy revising and retyping all of the stories for book form. Porter had agreed to write the introduction for the book, and Welty, Russell, and Doubleday were squabbling over the title of the collection. Finally, out of sheer exhaustion, they decided on the salesmen's choice, *A Curtain of Green and Other Stories*. Titles troubled Welty: "All my life I've been plagued by the inability to find a title for anything" (*More Conversations* 18). While she was preparing the stories for the final manuscript, she also found time to write new stories that take place at the Natchez Trace, including "The Winds" and "First Love." Both of these were bought by Mary Lou Aswell, an editor at *Harper's Bazaar,* marking the beginning of a supportive and lasting relationship between the two women.

Welty's successes gave her the chance to associate with other established writers—yet not all of these meetings resulted in friendships. For example, she met the ex-patriot Henry Miller the same year *A Curtain of Green* was accepted. Doubleday had commissioned Miller to travel around the U.S. and write about what he saw, and Woodburn wanted Welty to show him around Mississippi. The sexual frankness of Miller's *Tropic of Cancer* and *Tropic of Capricorn* had shocked many Americans; Welty and her friends were eager and curious to meet the writer behind the works. Before he arrived, Miller wrote Welty a letter, saying that if she needed the money, he could put her in touch with "an unfailing pornographic market" (*More Conversations* 220). When Welty's mother read the letter, she refused to allow Miller into the house. "Why I showed it to her I don't know," Welty said. "Anyway, she was so mad she wouldn't let him cross the threshold when he came here" (*More Conversations* 220). So Welty drove Miller around the county, but he was oblivious to the surroundings. She had trouble striking up conversation with him, and later she said he was not all like the bold and controversial man she and her friends were expecting, but was "the most boring business man you can imagine" (*Conversations* 202).

Even with her new successes and acquaintances, Welty never abandoned her Jackson friends. She continued to socialize with them, and lead a fairly quiet and modest life, living at home with her mother and spending her free time gardening. Waldron points out that Welty almost always mentioned gardening in her letters, and that a neighbor said later the only thing she remembered about Welty "was the frequency and fidelity with which both she and her mother worked outdoors" (129). During the different seasons, the yard at Pinehurst always bloomed with some kind of flower, whether camellias, daffodils, azaleas, roses, or irises.

As she enjoyed this quiet life, she also seized opportunities to enrich her writing career. In the summer of 1941 Welty spent two months at Yaddo, the famous artists' colony. Her mentor Katherine

Anne Porter, who would also be spending the summer there, had recommended her for the residency. Yaddo, located just outside Saratoga Springs, New York, was comprised of 500 acres and a 55 room graystone mansion where the artists were housed. The idea was that Welty would be given uninterrupted time and space to write; however, like Bread Loaf, Yaddo turned out to be a disappointment. With the attention placed on privacy and quietness, Welty found that she had trouble writing "Everything was so tense, even exalted" (*More Conversations*, 202). She stayed in a room with a sign posted on the door, "Silence. Writer at Work," and was too self-conscious to write anything.

In addition to her uneasiness in this writing space, she was also annoyed because her adversary, Carson McCullers, was also in residence. McCullers reportedly fell wildly in love with Porter, and Porter, not hiding her fear of lesbians or her dislike of McCullers, stuck even closer to Welty, as if this woman whom she viewed as young and innocent could act as a shield (Waldron 124). Waldron also points out that one reason Porter, who had been married several times and had many male lovers in her lifetime, felt comfortable around Welty was that, in regards to men, Porter did not view her as a competitor. Welty once told Caroline Gordon, the novelist and wife of the poet Allen Tate, that when she had confided to Porter that she was still a virgin, Porter had replied, "And you always will be" (qtd. in Waldron 104).

Porter convinced Yaddo's director to allow Welty to move in with her at North Farm, a few hundred yards from the main house where the other residents stayed. They spent most of their time together, with Welty chauffeuring them around in Porter's brand new Studebaker which Porter did not know how to drive. Welty enjoyed leaving the grounds and spending time in Saratoga Springs, attending the racetrack or shopping. Although she did not write any new stories while she was there, she managed to read the proofs to *A Curtain of Green*. Most of the time, over the duration of the two months, Welty was homesick, according to her friend John Robinson, and felt uncomfortable in the environment, even around Porter, who still had not written the introduction for *A Curtain of Green* (Waldron 126). Woodburn hounded Welty to remind Porter of the deadline, but Welty was too timid and polite to bother her.

In the end, Porter turned out the introduction just in time, and *A Curtain of Green* appeared in November. There was a publication party held in Greenwich Village which started at five p.m. and lasted well into the night. Welty's Jackson friends Frank Lyell and Hubert Creekmore attended, as well as Woodburn, and two artists she'd met at Yaddo—José de Creeft, a sculptor, and Karnig Nalbandian, an etcher. Welty, as usual, enjoyed her time in New York, attending art shows, the ballet, and concerts.

While *A Curtain of Green* sold only 7,000 copies in thirty years, the seventeen stories became widely known. The collection includes such widely regarded and anthologized stories as "Death of a Traveling Salesman," "Why I Live at the P.O. ," "A Petrified Man," "Powerhouse," and "A Worn Path." These early stories, influenced by Welty's travels around Mississippi, depict her sharp ear for dialogue and her persuasive sense of place, two characteristics which would become her trademarks. Some critics believe these early stories are "among the best Eudora ever wrote," and they have also been audience favorites; Welty read them aloud thousands of times over the period of her career (Waldron 117).

A Curtain of Green received mostly positive reviews. In *The Nation*, she was compared to the Russian writer Gogol, and Marianne Hauser in *The New York Times Book Review* wrote, "Few contemporary books have ever impressed me quite as deeply as this book" (qtd. in Waldron 130). However, *Time* complained about the focus on the "demented, the deformed, the queer, the highly spiced" (qtd. in Waldron 130). In these early stories, some of Welty's characters, similar to the characters of McCullers and Flannery O'Connor's, were mutes or disabled people, and many critics focused on this and labeled Welty as a Southern Gothic writer. Welty never liked the term Gothic, and did not feel it was accurate to compare the aforementioned writers' work with her own— especially McCullers.

WAR BREAKS OUT

After Pearl Harbor on December 7, 1941, Welty became active in the war effort, doing publicity for the Victory Book Campaign, the Red Cross, and the War Savings Committee. She visited New Orleans to see John Robinson, who was stationed there for a short time. Robinson and Welty shared literary interests; Robinson also loved to travel and explore. He was highly supportive of Welty's work, and she saw him as often as she could. When he was stationed overseas, she wrote him numerous letters.

As it did with many writers, the war atmosphere affected her energy to write—she was sadly watching her friends and brothers go off to war, and she found it difficult to tell a story. The war consumed her, and thirty years later, she tried to explain the way she felt:

> It's hard for young people today to conceive of how the country felt about the war. It was not like the Vietnam War in any respect. Everybody honestly believed we were trying to save the world from Nazism ... That was a terrible time to live through. I couldn't write about it, not at the time—it was too personal. I *could* write or translate things into domestic or other dimension in my writing, with the same things in mind. (*More Conversations* 66)

Although she did not write about the war, she was still working when she could, completing a few nonfiction articles and writing the Natchez Trace stories. She had published "The Wide Net," dedicated to Robinson, in *Harper's*, and wrote another story, one of her favorites, called "A Still Moment." Robinson, always supportive of Welty's writing, was especially drawn to these stories. He told a friend, "I'm very fond of all her Natchez Trace things—most of which are unpublished. She has made her own world there—and with what beauty and feeling—woods mostly, the birds" (qtd. in Waldron 140). She also won another O. Henry Prize and received a fellowship from the John Simon Guggenheim Foundation in 1942, in which she hoped the $1200 would allow her to devote herself to studying local history and researching the Natchez Trace trail.

While Welty devoted herself to war efforts and wrote whenever she could summon the energy, she continued to meet other writers, both established and new. For example, she received a phone call from Elizabeth Spencer, a senior at Belhaven, the college just across the street. Spencer was president of the college literary society, and she and her friends were surprised to learn that a published writer lived so close by. Spencer later said when she called, "one of the world's softest voices" answered the phone, and she was delighted Welty agreed to meet with the group (qtd. in Waldron 135). Welty struck up a friendship with Spencer and became a mentor to her; Spencer later went on to become a well-known novelist.

Meanwhile, in New York, Russell was working hard to sell *The Robber Bridegroom*. Finally, after already rejecting it once, Doubleday changed its mind and bought the manuscript. It was published as a novella on October 24, 1942. Welty went to the publication party in New York where she happily spent the O. Henry prize money on a record player and records.

The book received mixed reviews, with most reviewers perplexed by the fantasy and fairytale elements of the book. The critic Lionel Trilling reviewed the book in *The Nation*, calling it a "little fairy-tale novel" and dismissed the writing as precious: "nothing can be falser, more purple and 'literary' than conscious simplicity. This is prose whose eyes are a little too childishly wide; it is a little too conscious of doing something daring and difficult" (Turner 31). Yet despite the criticism, Welty's reputation grew steadily.

When Woodburn left Doubleday for Harcourt Brace, Welty, much to Doubleday's dismay, went with him. He promised to publish her eight Natchez Trace stories, which she had written in one of the most productive periods of her life. While it had taken six years to write the stories in *A Curtain of Green* and *The Robber Bridegroom*, she wrote the eight Trace stories in a year and a half, from January 1941 to the summer of 1942. Rich in symbolism, *The Wide Net* mixes realism, folklore, and legends of the Natchez Trace.

The Wide Net appeared in the fall of that year. Compared to *A Curtain of Green*, the book received mostly negative reviews. The critic Diana Trilling wrote a harsh review in the *Nation*: "Eudora Welty has developed her technical virtuosity to the point where it outweighs the uses to which it is put, and her vision of horror to the point of nightmare" (Turner 39). She continued, "In these new stories Miss Welty's prose constantly calls attention to herself and away from her object ... she is not only being falsely poetic, she is being untrue" (40). Welty admitted that Trilling's review, accusing of Welty of obscurity and showing off with language, affected her the most: "I was very hurt by that, and I was surprised. I don't think that it was true. I hope not. But I remember how sharply that cut" (*More Conversations* 293). One of Welty's supporters Robert Penn Warren wrote an eloquent response to Trilling in the *Kenyon Review*, claiming that Welty "has given us stories of brilliance and intensity; and as for the future, Miss Welty is a writer of great resourcefulness, sensitivity, and intelligence, and can probably fend for herself" (Turner 61).

Despite the mixed reviews, Welty won $1000 for *The Wide Net* from the American Academy of Arts and Letters. She also won another O. Henry first prize, making her the first author to receive two O. Henry first prizes in succession. She was happy with the success, but frustrated that she had not written anything new for months. She spent the days painting, gardening, playing records, and writing letters to Robinson. It had been eighteen months since she had sent a new story to her agent. Finally, she sent off the only piece she had completed called "The Delta Cousins." Editors rejected the story, claiming it was too long. Welty refused to cut the story, and then Russell told her the story looked like chapter two of a novel.

THE FIRST NOVEL

In 1944, Welty moved to New York for three months, hoping to work hard on "Delta Cousins," since she wasn't getting any writing done at home. She lived with a friend from Jackson, Rosa Wells, and picked up a job writing book reviews for *The New York Times Book Review*. Welty was a serious and thoughtful reviewer: "I didn't want to give a book a bad review. No matter what it is, it's a year out of somebody's life and they did the best they could" (*More Conversations* 218). While at the *Times*, she was also assigned to review books on the war, and used the pseudonym, Michael Ravenna, because one of the editors did not believe a southern lady should review wartime novels.

In October, she left the *Times* to return to Jackson, declining when the editor tried to persuade her to stay on. She suggested he hire her friend Nash Burger instead. After he accepted the job, Burger remained at the *Book Review* until he retired.

When Welty returned to Mississippi, she found new material for "Delta Cousins," thanks to John Robinson. He told Welty about the diaries of his great-great-grandmother, Nancy McDougall, who, from 1832 until 1879, filled up ten volumes of wide ledger books with diary entries. Welty drove up to the Delta to read the diaries, and their rich material provided historical background for her book.

What had started as a short story, "Delta Cousins," turned into *Delta Wedding*, Welty's first novel. The novel follows the Fairchild family and their life on the cotton plantation in the Mississippi Delta. The novel was comprised of historical facts and imaginative writing: "Nancy McDougall Robinson's journal provided background; memories of her own experiences added specificity to the action; and her imagination enlarged and enlivened" (Waldron 156). As the book grew, Welty sent off chapters to Robinson, now stationed overseas. She was writing the book to entertain him, without having a clear plan as how to write a novel.

Harcourt Brace bought *Delta Wedding* in 1945, and Edward Weeks at the Atlantic agreed to serialize the book in four installments, paying $1000 apiece for each of the four parts. The book appeared in April 1946, and sold well, the first 10,000 copy first printing selling out in less than a month. The reviews were mixed. Much to Welty's dismay, several reviewers compared it negatively to McCuller's *Member of the Wedding*, which appeared about the same time. In the *Nation*, Diana Trilling lambasted Welty for not criticizing the aristocratic, racist society that she portrayed. However, most critics praised her writing ability, and years later, the writer Reynolds Price described the novel as the "single most illuminating book we have about the fantastic complexity of racial relations in the Deep South" (qtd. in Waldron 164).

POSSIBLE ROMANCE

Welty's close friend John Robinson, discharged from the Army Air Corps, settled in San Francisco, and Welty went to visit in November 1946. Over the past few years, Welty and John had managed to meet up with each other quite frequently. Welty had visited him when he was stationed in New Orleans, St. Petersburg, Florida, and Harrisburg, Pennsylvania. When they could not see each other, they wrote each other. Most of John's letters, both to Welty and to friends, express pure admiration for her work and no romance. Although Waldron claims that a few friends thought they might marry, others said "there was never a romance," and Waldron admits it is difficult to access their feelings for each other (172). Welty's intensely guarded privacy makes it difficult for a biographer to know the extent of her romantic relationships; however, most people believe that she never had any sort of romance in her life, and that "Eudora's enduring relationship with Robinson appears to be as close as she ever came to romance with a man" (172).

Robinson also wrote short stories, but he did not publish until

Welty gave one of his stories to Max Perkins, who published the story in *The New Yorker*. Welty also shared her agent with Robinson; however, Russell had not sold any of his stories. So to earn a living, Robinson worked in a factory at night, and he wrote during the day. With this heavy work schedule, he seemed prone to sickness, and came down with a case of the flu, prolonging Welty's trip. She was worried about his health and state of mind.

Welty had intended to stay only for a few weeks in San Francisco, but ended up staying three months. She was quite seduced by the fog and ocean. She explored most of the Bay Area, and wrote several stories while in San Francisco, including "June Recital" and "Music from Spain." Different editors asked Welty to cut "June Recital," but she refused, and then her supporter Mary Lou Aswell, published it in *Harper's Bazaar*. Welty said admiringly of Aswell, "She was so good; she would keep the powers from cutting her fiction to make room for an ad, you know, that kind of thing. She fought for her writers" (*More Conversations* 186).

"Music From Spain," set in San Francisco, is one of only a half-dozen of her stories that takes place outside of Mississippi. Even in this non-Southern story, the imagery and setting details display Welty's power of description and close observation to the world around her. Most of her stories were set in the South because that was the place she knew best, and Mississippi was not only her source of inspiration, but her "source of knowledge" (*Conversations* 87).

Welty returned to the place she knew best in March, and continued to receive acknowledgement in the literary world. She was thrilled when the author E.M. Forester sent her a fan letter, stating that *The Wide Net* was full of "wild and lovely things" (qtd. in Waldron 178).

In the fall she was invited to the Northwest Writers' Conference at the University of Washington to give her first lecture. She spoke about the short story, using examples by Faulkner, Chekhov, Henry James, and Katherine Mansfield. She was anxious about speaking in front of an audience, but according to the attendees, she was the hit of the conference.

The $800 payment for the lecture financed another trip to San Francisco. Welty stayed for a couple of months, but this time when she returned to Jackson, according to Waldron, she seemed more disappointed with the West Coast. She wrote to Porter of her dislike of

San Francisco, then said it was probably her own fault she was not happy: "I was troubled a little in my life" (qtd. in Waldron 181). Waldron suspects she was "depressed that nothing much had come of her relationship with Robinson—no marriage, no real love affair" (181). This assumption cannot be validated; however, clearly Welty had some sort of special closeness with Robinson. Years later, Robinson would come to terms with his sexuality as a gay man.

A MOUNTAIN IN THE SOUTH

In the summer of 1948, Welty returned to New York for another extended stay. While she was there, she worked on writing a Broadway musical with the writer Hildegarde Dolson, also a client of Russell's. Welty, a great theater fan, enjoyed dabbling in this medium, although none of the skits went anywhere except one called "Bye-Bye, Brevoort." This skit became part of another revue, and was performed several times over the years. It was also later anthologized in *Plays in One Act*, edited by Daniel Halpern. Although Welty's contribution to theater was minor and somewhat forgettable, she liked experimenting in the genre. She was also working with Robinson, by mail, on adapting William Faulkner's *Sanctuary* for film. After they gave up on that idea, they turned to Welty's own book, *The Robber Bridegroom*, an idea that was also abandoned.

Although Welty often expressed an interest in writing for theater and film, she never seriously delved into the medium; she remained faithful to her true calling, fiction. For the past couple of years she had been working on short stories which she discovered were interrelated. When Welty wrote the story "Moon Lake," which drew on her memories of camp as a child, she realized that some of the characters from other stories were overlapping: "Quite suddenly I realized I was writing about the same people. All their interconnections came to light. That's what I mean by the fascinations of fiction: things that go on in the back of your mind, that gradually emerge" (*Conversations* 43). The book began to take shape: it would be a collection of seven interconnected stories that take place in the imaginary small town of Morgana in the Mississippi Delta.

Harcourt Brace bought the book, *The Golden Apples*, and Welty retyped the stories for publication, with help from her brother Walter's wife, Mittie, and John Robinson, who tried to keep her from further rewriting. Although Welty did not revise her earliest stories, her techniques had changed over the years, and now she admitted she often revised considerably: "I do an awful lot of it" (*More Conversations* 309).

The Golden Apples, published in 1949, received positive reviews. The stories, rich with modernist techniques, interested academic critics for the allusions to myths and references to Yeats's poem "The Song of the Wandering Aengus." For critics, this book was perhaps her most memorable: "All of Miss Welty's gifts for compression, metaphorical language and poetic structure were on display" (Krebs 4). *The Golden Apples* was also Welty's personal favorite. She was fascinated by the interconnections in the stories, and felt fond of the characters: "I loved everybody in *The Golden Apples*. The good ones and the bad, the happy ones and the sad ones. I loved them all" (*More Conversations* 85).

That summer Welty finally had the chance to meet William Faulkner, a fellow Mississippian writer whom she greatly admired. A few years earlier, he had sent her an encouraging letter about The *Robber Bridegroom*, telling her, "You're doing *all right*" (*More Conversations* 221). She had never thought she would meet him, but that summer, the grand dame of Oxford society, Miss Ella Somerville, invited Welty and John Robinson for a visit. Faulkner was there, and Welty immediately liked him. She said he was kind, and friendly. After dinner, they sang hymns and folksongs. Welty and Faulkner talked quite a bit, but not once about writing. The next morning, Faulkner invited Welty and Robinson to go sailing on his 19-foot sloop, the *Ring Dove*, on Lake Sardis. The man-made lake was marshy and swampy, and they had to wade out to Faulkner, already in the sailboat. Welty, unprepared, wore a cotton dress and white pumps, and she was petrified of sailing. But she went, of course. Faulkner didn't say a word the entire time and "it just felt like a dream going all around" (*More Conversations* 181).

Welty had always admired Faulkner's work. For many years his work was not available in Jackson, and she had to buy the books whenever she was in New Orleans. "I was naturally in the deepest awe and reverence of him," she said, and stressed that she never felt that she was in competition with him (*Conversations* 79). Instead, living in the same state as Faulkner was "like living near a big mountain, something majestic—it made me happy to know it was there, all that worked of his life. But it wasn't a helping or hindering presence. Its magnitude, all by itself, made it something remote in my own working life. When I thought of Faulkner it was when I *read*" (*Conversations* 80). She often praised Faulkner's skill with dialogue: "What I learned from Faulkner about speech was more important than any of those other things—it's that our rhythms in the South are different ... The times we breathe in a sentence or don't breathe—they come in different places. Our phrasings and rhythms show how we think" (*Conversations* 280).

Welty learned to write both by observing the world around her and by reading; the writers that influenced her spanned a wide spectrum: Greek and Roman poetry, history and fables, Austen, Shakespeare, Milton, Dante, Tolstoy and Dostoevsky, 18th century English, and 19th century French novelists. She adored folk tales, fairy tales, legends, and the songs and stories of her people. She was a big fan of W.B. Yeats and Virginia Woolf. *To The Lighthouse* had a particularly strong influence on Welty: "[Woolf] was the one who opened the door. When I read *To the Lighthouse*, I felt, Heavens, what is this? I was so excited by the experience I couldn't sleep or eat" (*Conversations* 75). Not everything she liked was so literary; Welty also loved mysteries, including books by Dick Frances and Ross Macdonald. Once she even wrote Macdonald a fan letter, but never mailed it, afraid, she stated in an interview, "he'd think it—icky" (*Conversations* 32). Macdonald read the interview and then sent Welty a fan letter, and the two became friends.

Welty never studied with a particular writer, or attended a writing program. Although Porter served as an informal mentor to Welty early in her career, Welty stated: "I was always my own teacher" (*OWB* 93). In the introduction to *A Curtain of Green*, Porter confirmed this philosophy: "She has never studied the writing craft in any college. She has never belonged to a literary group, and until after her first collection was ready to be published she had never discussed with any colleague or older artist any problem of her craft" (Porter 152). Welty was too shy to show her work to her friends or supporters until she believed it was absolutely finished and polished.

INTIMATE RELATIONSHIPS

Welty won another Guggenheim fellowship for $2500. This prize, combined with the $5000 advance for *Golden Apples*, provided her with enough money to travel to Europe. This would be her first trip overseas;

she was now forty years old. She went by ship, securing a space on the *Italia*, which sailed from New York on October 14, 1949, and reached Genoa a couple of weeks later. She stayed in Genoa for a few weeks, then took a train to Paris, where she stayed in the Hotel des Saints-Peres on the Left Bank and soaked up the sights of the city, attending the Louvre, the Luxembourg Gardens, and Notre Dame. She visited her friend Mary Lou Aswell, and then when Robinson arrived in Florence on a Fulbright fellowship, Welty returned to Italy to spend time with him. From there, Welty traveled to London to visited friends and meet more writers, including Henry Yorke, the novelist who wrote under the name of Henry Green, an author she greatly admired.

Next she went to Dublin where she called on Elizabeth Bowen, the Anglo-Irish novelist whose work she admired. She admitted later, "Well, I had never in my life looked up anybody that I didn't know. But it kept tempting me, like a fantasy almost" (*More Conversations* 102). Elizabeth Bowen was the author of *The Last September*, *The Hotel*, *The House in Paris*, and *The Death of the Heart*. She had reviewed *A Curtain of Green* in England, praising the work. While Welty was in Paris, she heard from someone that Bowen wanted to meet her. Elizabeth immediately invited Welty to Bowen's Court, her ancestral home in Southern Ireland, and there an important and intimate friendship began.

Waldron describes Bowen as "a striking woman. She was tall and large-boned, her copper hair pulled tightly back" (Waldron 150). She was intelligent and beautiful, and a prominent figure in the British literary world. She married Alan Cameron, but according to Waldron, had both male and female lovers, including the poet May Sarton.

Bowen enjoyed meeting Welty, describing her as "quiet, self-contained, easy, outwardly old-fashioned, very funny indeed when she starts talking" (qtd. in Waldron 210). They spent the afternoons walking the grounds or taking wild drives, with Bowen speeding and usually driving on the wrong side of the road. In the evenings, friends joined them, and they drank whiskey and played cards. The two women developed a close friendship which would continue for the rest of their lives. Welty felt a kinship with Bowen; she reminded Welty of a Southerner, with her talkative personality and congeniality.

When Welty returned to Jackson, she left almost immediately to visit Mary Lou Aswell in New York, who was separating from her husband Fritz Peters. Aswell would later leave the New York publishing scene and move to New Mexico with a woman lover. Welty wrote to a friend that she was "tired and depressed" (qtd. in Waldron 214). Waldron assumes that "John Robinson was the cause, although she must have known for some time that her relationship with him would be no more than platonic" (214). Robinson had acknowledged his sexuality, and was in Italy with his lover, Enzo Rocchigiani, with whom he would spend the rest of his life. Although Robinson and Welty remained good friends, the separation must have deeply hurt her: "What Eudora's feelings were toward him remain a mystery," attests Waldron, "but it is impossible not to believe that when he turned to Rocchigiani, it was a great loss for her" (214).

In the spring of 1951, Welty returned to Europe, using a $1250 advance for an unwritten book of short stories from Harcourt Brace to finance the trip. She stayed alone in Elizabeth Bowen's second house near Regent's Park where she hoped to get a substantial amount of writing done. She actually spent most of her time looking out the window. Then she went to Bowen's Court in April to visit Elizabeth. She had already seen Bowen since that first trip to Ireland—the previous spring, Bowen had made her first trip to the U.S. in 17 years, and stayed with Welty and her mother in Mississippi.

At Bowen's Court, the two women worked in the mornings, met around eleven o'clock for a sherry, returned to work, and then met up for lunch. Bowen told a friend: "Eudora Welty is staying in the house—working away at one of her great short stories in another room. This is ideal: I'm so fond of her, and her preoccupation during the day with her own work gives me a freedom unknown when one has an ordinary guest" (qtd. in Waldron 219). Welty was drawn to Bowen's intelligent mind, her friendly personality, and her ardor for life: "She was a marvelous lady, a responsive person, you know, to mood and place, and she was so happy, so delighted by things in life. And very apprehensive too. It was an Irishness, a sense of your surroundings, very sensitive to what you can feel all the time" (*More Conversations* 101).

Welty wrote "The Bride of Innisfallen" and it was her first piece of fiction that was published in the *New Yorker*. After Ireland, Welty traveled in England and spent time in London, one of her favorite places.

After Welty returned to Jackson, she and Bowen continued to keep up their friendship, and would remain friends until Bowen's death of lung cancer on February 22, 1973. Waldron states that, as with

Robinson, Welty's relationship with Bowen remained ambiguous. Welty's numerous and loving letters reveal she was "ardent and full of wonder" in regards to Bowen (Waldron 225). After the most recent trip to Ireland, she wrote Bowen a letter of gratitude: "You were sweet ... you did so much—but I let you, loved it and took my pleasure, I let you as I love you ... I'll never, never forget any of those days and nights ... I wish I had known all my life of this visit, and could have known the anticipation ... (qtd. in Waldron 221). Their relationship caused some speculation and gossip: "No one knows the truth about Welty's sexuality. Most of her men friends—John Robinson, Hubert Creekmore, Frank Lyell, Lehman Engel, Reynolds Price—were gay, as were many of her women friends. She has always refused to say anything at all about her private life, despite the many interviews she has given" (Waldron 225). Regardless of the exact nature of their relationship, it is clear the two were very close. Welty felt a kinship with her that was not as apparent in her other friendships. She once talked about the differences in Elizabeth Bowen and her other longtime friend, Katherine Anne Porter, and how she felt closer to Bowen's personality: "I enjoy people, and I think there's a great difference in that respect between Katherine Anne and Elizabeth. Katherine Anne might enjoy having a circle around her, but there she really remained with in herself. Elizabeth was the opposite; she was an in-taker. She just took everything in. She was curious and fascinated by most people she met, and she really wanted to know" (*More Conversations* 108).

PUBLICATIONS, AWARDS, HONORS

During 1952–1953, Eudora Welty continued entertaining guests in her home, traveling to New York City, receiving awards, and publishing stories. She met Robert Penn Warren for the first time in person when he spoke at Millsaps College. She also spent time with Porter, and entertained P.H. Newby, a novelist and BBC writer. At Mississippi State College for Women, she met the poet Randall Jarrell, who described her as "one of the three or four nicest writers I've ever met—somewhat homely, but so sympathetic, natural, and generally attractive that you quite forget it, particularly since you feel you've known her always" (Waldron 227).

The *New Yorker* editor William Maxwell bought Welty's stories "Kin" and "No Place for You, My Love." Maxwell was an important supporter-editor of Welty's. In January of 1953 Welty met with him to show him the story she'd been working on tentatively titled "Uncle Daniel." She read it out loud to him and he "laughed so hard that he cried" (Waldron 230). Eventually, this long story turned into a humorous novel called *The Ponder Heart*, a story about a mentally retarded man named Uncle Daniel, as narrated by a character named Edna Earle.

The *New Yorker* paid $7,700 for serial rights, and Harcourt Brace agreed to a $5000 advance and set publication for January, 1954. When *The Ponder Heart* appeared, it received mainly positive reviews. What this book also accomplished was to shine the local spotlight on her. Although many Mississippians were aware of Welty, not many had read her work until this publication. *The Ponder Heart* began to lift her status to a local, and treasured, celebrity. She received fan mail, with people thanking her for writing about their own Uncle Ponder.

Welty continued to be showered with successes. She was elected to the National Institute of Arts and Letters, along with Tennessee Williams and Carson McCullers. She received an honorary degree from the University of Wisconsin. That same year Fulbright invited her to spend six weeks at an American Studies Conference at Cambridge University in England. At first she hesitated, nervous about the required lectures and teaching, but then she accepted the honor and worked on preparing one of the lectures which would eventually be published as her famous essay, "Place in Fiction."

Welty was the first woman to be invited to a Fulbright conference, and she was also the first woman to ever cross the threshold into the Hall at Peterhouse College where they held a special dinner:

> They were so dear the way they told me: they said, 'Miss Welty, you are invited to come to this, but we must tell you that we debated for a long time about whether or not we should ask you. No woman has ever crossed the threshold, including Queen Victoria, who *demanded* to and was refused.' And I thought, well now, what would be the correct thing for me to do, they having given me this leave? And then I thought, I'm going to do it. They've already decided that I can, and I think to back out would sort of demean the *greatness*, the *momentousness*, of this invitation. Besides, I was curious. (*More Conversations* 107)

Welty crossed the threshold, and during dinner, the port and cigars were passed to her just as they were the men. Welty was well-liked by her students and the other conference attendees. "At first sight she was not an attractive woman, but the minute she began to talk that did not matter," said one person. "She was lively and witty and I felt as though I had known her all my life. She was full of curiosity" (qtd. in Waldron 238). In her free time, Welty had lunch with E.M. Forester, and she also saw Monk's House, Virginia Woolf's country home.

Back in the States, she agreed to more college visits and lectures, in order to supplement her income. One of these lectures was scheduled at Duke University. Because she knew she would arrive at the Durham train in the middle of the night, she politely requested that nobody from the college meet her. However, when she stepped off the train, the town was pitch dark, and she was worried about how she would get to a hotel. Then she saw "this slim, young man in a white suit standing all alone on the platform" (*More Conversations* 241). This stranger was the author Reynolds Price, then a senior at Duke. Welty later liked to say that when she stepped onto the platform, she "couldn't see anything that night except a savior dressed in white" (*More Conversations* 180).

BRIGHT LIGHTS OF BROADWAY

The next two years, 1955 and 1956, were a busy and promising time for Welty. *The Bride of Innisfallen*, a collection of stories she had been writing for the past five years, was published. Several of these stories were set outside of the South. Although most of her fiction took place in Mississippi, she was not confined to this region, either in her fiction or sensibilities, and the critic Ruth Vande Kieft points out that "for all of her attachment to Mississippi, Eudora Welty has also shown a detachment, a broadness of perspective, that comes from both her personal history and her temperament" (9). However, in order to write stories that took place outside of Mississippi, Welty explained, "I had to write every one of them from the point of view of the traveler or the outsider" (*Conversations* 329).

She received her second honorary degree (which would be one of many), this one from a small college called Western College for Women in Ohio, and she was awarded the William Dean Howells Medal from the National Academy of Arts and Letters for *The Ponder Heart*. Not much later, two playwrights, Joe Fields and Jerry Chodorov, wrote Welty asking if they could adapt the novel for the stage.

Welty, who loved theater, looked forward to this revival of her novel. However, she was disappointed with the first draft, and, gently, she suggested changes. After nine months of revisions and rewrites, the production came together. Welty was still quite pessimistic and worried about the play. It opened in New York on February 16, 1956. Welty was there, along with many of her friends, including Russell, Maxwell, Creekmore, and Aswell. Her reactions to the play were mixed. The playwrights had changed the importance of Edna Earle; instead of narrating the story, she was now in the background. Welty was also startled to hear lines from her other stories quoted in the play. However, by the end of the night, she warmed to the production: "There were times I thought I was in the wrong theater, that perhaps my book was being done as a play in another theater down the street.... But the actors and other folks were so warm, so kind.... I went back to see it three or four times" (*Conversations* 151). After a summer of many parties and social occasions—in which she spent time with her Jackson friends Hubert Creekmore and Frank Lyell, the three of them now in their late forties—Welty had the chance to see her novel performed in her hometown. The Jackson Little Theater opened its season with a production of *The Ponder Heart*. The *Jackson Daily News* columnist Frank Hains directed and rewrote the play from the point of view of Edna Earle, and Welty thought this version stayed closer to the original.

TROUBLES AT HOME

Welty's seemingly good fortune had another darker, sadder side to it, which became most apparent from 1956 to 1966, a decade that nearly consumed her and her writing—indeed, *The Bride of Innisfallen* would be her last published book for fifteen years.

Chestina Welty, Welty's mother, was often exhausting and demanding. Once, for example, when Porter came in town for a visit, Welty wanted to invite her to dinner, but first had to ask her mother. Porter was outraged that a forty-two year old woman had to ask her mother's permission to entertain house guests. Welty rarely complained, but she once said to a friend, Robert Drake, "You see how it is. I can't leave home whenever I like" (qtd. in Waldron 254). Although Chestina was often overbearing, she was also quite proud of Welty's honors and achievements. After all, it was her mother who encouraged her to use her imagination, and who introduced her to the world of literature. Welty said that her mother was "very proud of my work, because she was a *reader*. She loved the written word" (*More Conversations* 147).

Yet her mother demanded attention, and as her health declined, Chestina only grew more difficult and irascible. Her eyesight worsened until she could no longer read, and she went to New Orleans to undergo surgery, an event later recorded in Welty's novel *The Optimist's Daughter*. Welty felt it was her sole responsibility to care for her mother—her "principal care and burden, sapping her energy for nearly eleven years" (Waldron 253).

To make the situation more exacerbating, it was not just her mother's poor health and difficult personality that consumed Welty. The health of both brothers was also declining. Edward, the one whom she was closest in age, suffered from emotional problems. A successful architect with the Jackson firm R.W. Naef for sixteen years, Edward suddenly left the job and went off on his own. Although Welty, always very private, never publicly spoke of his problems, she mentioned in letters to friends her brother's "mental problems" (Waldron 217). As Edward battled with these ambiguous emotional troubles, the physical health of her youngest brother, Walter, was quickly failing. Walter, who like his father worked in the insurance business, suffered from extreme arthritis, and his health quickly deteriorated. He checked into clinics and hospitals, and Welty often cared for his daughters so that his wife Mittie could be with him. Between watching her nieces, worrying over her brothers, and caring for her mother, Welty had very little time for herself or her writing.

In the moments when it seemed like everyone's health was improving and Welty could take a break from her role as caretaker, she spent time with friends. Once in the spring she was fortunate enough to get away for a short trip to New York City, where she attended a party of the dancer Martha Graham—Welty greatly admired Graham's work. New York was a much needed distraction from the distress at home. However, Walter's health worsened. He had trouble focusing his eyes and standing upright. The doctors explained he had heart troubles, but didn't know how to treat him; at one point he was taking 59 pills a day.

According to Waldron, "As family illnesses kept Welty from

writing, she began, at forty-nine, to doubt her own existence" (258). So when Bryn Mawr College invited her to be the Lucy Martin Donnelly Fellow at the college from 1958-1959, in which she would receive $3,000 for the year without any teaching requirements, she quickly accepted. She was stepping out of the family turmoil and into the literary world once more. She also served as an unpaid honorary consultant in American letters at the Library of Congress, and while in Washington, read to an excited crowd. Three Washington papers ran stories on her, and *The Daily News* reporter Tom Kelly wrote, "Miss Eudora Welty, as shy and southern as a mocking bird, was in Our Town yesterday, whistling Dixie in a new and gentle way" (qtd. in Waldron 259). This brief period was an open window; however, the turn of events did not last long.

Welty was called away from Bryn Mawr to return to Jackson. Her brother Walter, forty-three years old, died on January 9, 1959. Welty did not speak publicly about her grief, nor did she lean on the shoulders of her friends. As usual, she was reticent and withdrawn about personal matters and never lost her composure.

A few months later Welty returned to Bryn Mawr, but the visit was quite short—her mother's health troubles called her back to Jackson. After Walter's death, Chestina's frail health continued to deteriorate. Seventy-six years old, she went in and out of the hospital, and when she was at home, she suffered from blackouts. Welty stayed with her as much as possible, and bore the responsibility of caring for her mother full-time, leaving herself with no physical or mental energy to write or to find work. No new money was coming in, and the significant financial burden quickly increased. Although Welty hired home-nurses, she still felt that she could not leave her mother alone. She even turned down a $7500 grant from the Ford Foundation to study playwriting at the Phoenix Theater and the Actors Studio in New York. She also did not accept the invitation to be one of the distinguished American artists and writers at John F. Kennedy's inauguration in January 1961. Her friends were worried about her financial and emotional situation. Creekmore mentioned her unusual "arid attitude of doing nothing" about work or writing (qtd. in Waldron 263).

Chestina grew unpredictable and irrational; sometimes she would refuse to talk to her granddaughters when they visited. She often railed against Welty; whenever she went into the hospital, for example, she became furious at Welty. The doctors advised a nursing home, but Welty refused. During all of this time she "continued faithfully to look after her mother and never, over the course of all those years, displayed the slightest bitterness, regret, or self-pity. She might complain of being depressed or lament that she had not time to write, but these remarks were made almost in passing" (Waldron 263). Welty's only alleviation were the short trips she took to Washington or New York, or the time she spent with friends: "It is impossible to overestimate how much good friends meant to Welty. All her life she cultivated friendships as she did her camellias, and the friends reciprocated with unstinting approval and support" (Waldron 265).

GROWING FINANCIAL BURDENS

Although she felt obligated to stay in Jackson caring for her mother, Welty also needed to earn some kind of income. As she once said, "Earning a living is a very big question when you are a writer. You don't know how, when, where, or if" (*Conversations* 340). She never warmed to the idea of lecturing, but this was a fairly easy way to earn money. She went to Smith College in Northampton, Massachusetts, to be the William Allen Neilson Professor, in which she was required to give three public lectures. She recycled "Place in Fiction" from her lecture in Cambridge and "Short Stories" from the very first conference in Seattle, and wrote a new one, "Words into Fiction." This stay gave her a much needed break from the events at home; now she had more time to write, and she was pleased to find out that her mother had done fine in her absence. She then attended the Southern Literary Conference at Converse College in South Carolina, where for the first time she met Flannery O'Connor. The two Southern authors were equally pleased to meet each other. Welty admired O'Connor's work: "I think she was a fantastically gifted writer. I have enjoyed everything she has done. I love it" (*Conversations* 20), and O'Connor praised Welty: "I really liked Eudora Welty ... [she was] just a real nice woman" (qtd. in Waldron 266). When Welty returned to Jackson and met up with her friends, they all thought she looked better, and were relieved to find out that she planned on going away in the fall.

   However, at the end of the summer, another set back occurred: Chestina fell and broke her hip, and was confined to a wheel chair for six months. Eventually, Welty gave in to the doctor's advice and moved her mother to a nursing home in Yazoo City, forty-five miles away. Welty always felt guilty about moving her mother to a nursing home, believing that she had disappointed and betrayed her.

The responsibility to earn money continued to fall heavily on Welty's shoulders. She wrote a children's book, *The Shoe Bird*, to bring in a little money. She also worked the college circuit; instead of giving lectures, she usually gave readings. Between traveling to colleges and the nursing home to see her mother, Welty was extremely busy and she found little time to write. Waldron explains the college visits drained her, yet she needed them for survival: "She needed the money that came from college visits, but they created a viscous circle; because she had no time to write, her income fell, so she traveled more to college campuses and had even less time to write" (270).

Colleges welcomed Welty: she was gracious and courteous, and never caused trouble by getting drunk or making passes at students, as other writers were known to do. The visits also offered time away from her exhausting life in Jackson and gave her a chance to socialize with other literary folk. "In a sense these visits provided her with an emotional life of some kind in the absence of husband, children, or lover" (Waldron 270). While she visited, she also agreed to discussion groups, autographs, and social events. A professor from Vassar, William Gifford, stated, "She was so gentle, the kindest person. She talked about her experiences in writing and asked the students about their experiences" (qtd. in Waldron 271). She was devoted and patient. However, Welty hated leaving her mother behind. She needed to find a way to stay closer to home.

Although Welty had never wanted to be a teacher and had turned down many offers, the desperate need for money motivated her to ask Millsaps College about the possibility of a teaching position; the local college was of course delighted and quickly created a position. Welty admired teachers from her own childhood, and many of her characters were teachers. However, she did not feel she had the expertise: "As certain as I was of wanting to be a writer, I was certain of *not* wanting to be a teacher. I lacked the instructing turn of mind, the selflessness, the patience for teaching, and I had the unreasoning feeling that I'd be trapped" (*OWB* 89). She also did not believe that fiction writing could be taught, and was suspect of workshops. Her class at Millsaps differed from the typical creative writing class. Welty assigned readings and discussed literature, and she told the students they could write stories if they wanted to, but she set no deadlines. She even read some of her own work-in-progress to the class. Later, when an interviewer asked her about this job, she was modest about what she actually did at Millsaps, "I never was a teacher, I'll tell you that" (*More Conversations* 169).

CIVIL RIGHTS

While Welty struggled to take care of her ailing mother, tensions rose in Jackson over issues of civil rights, racism, and integration; although all her life Welty would make it clear that being an artist was not the same as being an activist, she was certainly affected by the heated mood of her home town and the historical events of the fifties and sixties.

In May 1954, the United States Supreme Court made the historic ruling in *Brown v. Board of Education*, to outlaw segregation in public schools. Mississippi resisted for years; in Jackson, soon after the ruling, the White Citizens Council went from door to door trying to recruit new members—Welty, like her friends, was appalled, but they were in the minority. Hubert Creekmore wrote, "Mississippi is disgusting and frightening with its segregation fanaticism and I'll be glad to get away from it" (qtd. in Waldron 242).

Nearly a decade later, tempers in Jackson were boiling at the forced integration of the University of Mississippi. Welty was horrified by the racist and conservative attitudes, but she was also quite wrapped up in personal family troubles. Then in the summer of 1963, Medgar Evers, the NAACP's civil rights leader in Jackson, was shot and killed by an unidentified killer. Flooded with anger, Welty wrote her famous story "Where Is the Voice Coming From?" in one sitting. She explained: "There was one story that anger certainly lit the fuse.... But all that absorbed me, though it started as outrage, was the necessity I felt for entering into the mind and inside the skin of a character who could hardly have been more alien or repugnant to me" (*OWB* 43). The story, written in the first point-of-view, is a chilling reconstruction of what Welty imagined ran through the mind of the man who killed Evers. Welty sent the story to Maxwell, and he quickly bought it and rushed the story into print in the *New Yorker*. Before the story ran, the real killer, Byron de la Beckwith, was arrested for the murder. Welty had been right about so many of the details (except for his socio-economic class—in a reference to Faulkner, Welty said she had thought the murderer was a "Snopes," when really he was a "Compson"), that Welty had to spend time with editors over the phone, changing times and makes of cars, in order to avoid a libel suit.

A newspaper reporter from New York called Welty to find out if she had suffered any repercussions for writing the story:

> Had anybody burned a cross on my lawn, he wanted to know. I told him, No, of course not, and he wanted to know if he could call back in a few days, 'in case anything develops.' I told him I couldn't see any sense in his running up his phone bill. The people who burn crosses on lawns don't read me in *The New Yorker*. Really, don't people know the first thing about the South? (*Conversations* 31)

Welty was annoyed with Northerners assumptions and simplistic observations about the South. She also strongly felt that a novelist was not responsible to write about politics, and thought that much of the political fiction that was being published was not very good. She made this case clear in a lecture for Millsaps, which was also published in the *Atlantic* as "Must the Novelist Crusade?" This essay was Welty's answer to the critics who accused her of ignoring the civil rights movement:

> We cannot in fiction set people to acting mechanically or carrying placards to make their sentiments plain. People are not Right and Wrong, Good and Bad, Black and White personified; flesh and blood and the sense of comedy object. Fiction writers cannot be tempted to make the mistake of looking at people in the generality—that is to say, of seeing people as not at all like us. If human beings are to be comprehended as real, then they have to be treated as real, with minds, hearts, memories, habits, hopes, with passions and capacities like ours. This is why novelist begin the study of people from within. (*Short Essays, and Memoir* 806)

For the rest of her life, she would stick by this sentiment, as over and over again she would be asked to defend her position. Welty had faith that personal relationships were stronger weapons against racism than political rallies. Tired of the late night phone calls from Northerners harassing her for living in Mississippi, she stopped listing her phone number. She once explained: "All my life I've been opposed to such things as racism and injustice and cruelty ... Whatever wrongs there are, I want my stories to show them as they are, to let them speak for themselves. I don't want to preach, I'll leave that to the editorial writers and essayists" (*Conversations* 151). She cited Steinbeck as a writer she believed crusaded in his fiction and thus "bores [her] so" (*More Conversations* 226).

Yet, these feelings did not stop her writing a second story about civil rights almost a year after "Where Is the Voice Coming From?" It was the hot, steamy summer of 1964, and young civil rights leaders from all over the country had converged in Mississippi to rally and demonstrate. White Mississippians resisted, leading to the tragic murder of three CORE workers in Philadelphia, Mississippi. Eventually, the summer's protests and demonstrations led to the passage of the Voting Rights Act of 1965. Welty, weary and exhausted from the town's unending racial turmoil, wrote a story which went on to be published in the *New Yorker* and then won an O. Henry prize. She claimed "The Demonstrators" was not primarily a civil rights story, even though it dealt with those issues:

> Well, all of it was a reflection of society at the time it happened. Every story in effect does that.... They all reflect the way we were deeply troubled in that society and within ourselves at what was going on in the sixties. They reflect the effect of change sweeping all over the South—of course, over the rest of the country too, but I was writing about where I was living and the complexity of those changes. (*Conversations* 259)

Welty was not opposed to writing about the problems of segregation and racism, however, she wanted the stories to be addressed them from the point of the view of "the human, not the political" (*Conversations* 166).

AFTER A LONG SILENCE

The bitterness between blacks and whites continued to escalate in Jackson, Mississippi, and at home, the health of her mother and brother continued to decline. Whenever Welty could find any scraps of time or energy, she worked on what she called the "reunion novel." She showed part of it to Russell and he thought the book was ready to send to publishers. Welty was hesitant; she was fearful that people would criticize her for not writing about the civil rights struggle. She continued to work on the novel in bits and pieces, even as everything around her fell apart. Sometimes while she was driving to the nursing home, she would write down ideas for her novel with her right hand, while steering with her left.

In the fall of 1965, her brother Edward, also suffering from arthritis, broke his neck, and then on Thanksgiving Day, her mother had a stroke that left her comatose. Chestina no longer spoke and rarely recognized Welty. Welty was exhausted and probably depressed. She made trips to the nursing home to see her mother and to the hospital to see her brother, not wanting either one to find out the other was sick. Although she rarely talked about her private life, she did mention the emotional exhaustion and complexity of this experience: "Neither one knew the other was so terribly ill ... [Edward] was in a hospital there and [my mother] was in a hospital in Yazoo City, and I was going back and forth trying to keep each one from knowing the other was so terribly ill" (*More Conversations* 141).

Then, on January 20, 1966, Chestina Welty died. Her death brought Welty a mix of terrible grief and alleviation: "It lifted an enormous burden from Eudora, but left her, as the deaths of close family members often do, to deal what her conflicted feelings of grief and guilt" (Waldron 282). Unfortunately, the loss did not stop with the death of her mother: four days later, Edward died unexpectedly. Welty was left alone, the last of her family. She was fifty-seven years old.

"The deaths, so close together, of a strong mother and a beloved brother must have meant a bereavement beyond endurance," Waldron speculates (282). Welty did not speak publicly of her grief. She, as always, was stoic and indefatigable, and returned to the duties of lectures within a month. Six months later her good friend Hubert Creekmore (also brother of her sister-in-law Mittie), died in New York, and Welty was shattered again.

With the deaths of her brother and mother, Welty was left alone in the house on Pinehurst Street, the last living of the family of five. For almost fifteen years, from the mid 50's to the late 60's, she had published only a few short stories, book reviews, and a children's book, as she spent all of her time caring for family: "Some writers have speculated that she seemed also to be undergoing some sort of ordeal of the spirit or artistic crisis" (Krebs 5). One way that Welty possibly found a way to deal with her grief was to put aside the "reunion novel" and turn to something more personal.

The result was the slim and subtle novel *The Optimist's Daughter*, first published in the *New Yorker*. The protagonist's mother, Becky McKelva, is clearly based on Welty's mother. Although Welty fiercely resisted the idea that any of her fiction was autobiographical, she admitted that this novel contained elements of the truth: "It's the first thing I've ever done that has direct autobiographical information in it. I'm not sure that was right—the mother is based on my mother. The boys are her brothers—I think I may have added an extra one—and the West Virginia part is set in her own country" (*More Conversations* 69). The novel allowed her to revisit her own childhood memories, remembering the trips she took to West Virginia to visit her mother's family, and also helped her come to terms with the losses and grief. She said that the novel was a way to resolve something after her mother's death: "The feeling of the daughter who can't help, you know, who wants to understand and help—it's removed in different stages and in different parts of the story. My emotions are in that book, my true emotions. You can't make those up, don't want to make them up" (*More Conversations* 139).

Aside from magazine publications, Welty had not published a book in fifteen years, and her fans had been eagerly awaiting something new. While Welty had spent time caring for her family and traveling to colleges to earn an income, she also worked on, in bits and pieces, the "reunion novel." It took her at least ten years to write. When she turned to *The Optimist's Daughter*, she packed all of the pages of the reunion novel in boxes, and finally one day she sat down and read through everything, and discovered she just may have a novel. "And the fact that it stayed alive in my head over a period of years cheered me up because I thought that it must have some spark of vitality or it would have just faded away," she explained. "But it kept staying with me; I only kept thinking of more and more scenes. So then when I did have time to work on it, I just had boxes full of scenes" (*Conversations* 47).

The revision process for this novel was complicated and in-depth. She drew a map of the house, in order to keep track of the many characters moving around. She threw away pages, and with the remaining ones, she cut and pinned them together, revising with scissors and pins: "Pasting is too slow and you can't undo it, but with pins you can move things from anywhere to anywhere, and that's what I really love doing—putting things in their best and proper place, revealing things at the time where they matter most. Often I shift things from the very beginning to the very end. Small things—one face, one word—but things important to me" (*Conversations* 89). The novel, set in the thirties, depicts a poor white family in Northeast Mississippi gathered to celebrate Granny Vaughn's 90th birthday, and is nearly entirely comprised of only dialogue and action.

Harcourt Brace did not express enthusiasm about publishing the novel, so she withdrew the manuscript, along with *The Optimist's Daughter*, and Russell sent them both to Random House. Albert Erskine, who had helped discover Welty's stories at the *Southern Review* in the 1930's, paid the $50,000 advance for which Welty was asking.

Losing Battles, her first book in fifteen years, became a bestseller almost as soon as it appeared. Welty, sixty-one years old, was delighted. Many critics provided tributes to Welty's long and admirable writing career, and the book was nominated for the National Book Award (although Saul Bellow's *Mr. Sammler's Planet* would win). *Time* magazine chose it as one of the top ten books of the year, and it was awarded the Edward McDowell Medal.

LOCAL CELEBRITY

The early seventies brought Welty many awards and honors, and her reputation grew quickly, on both local and national levels. In 1972, she was appointed by President Nixon to a six-year term on the National Council on the Arts, in which she received a hundred dollars a day plus traveling expenses. A year later she received Gold Medal for the Novel from the National Institute of Arts and Letters, which was awarded only once every ten years. The last award had gone to William Faulkner—and Welty had been the one to present it to him.

About a hundred of her photographs from her WPA days were collected and published by Random House in *One Time, One Place: Mississippi in The Depression, a Snapshot Album*. Critics admired the book, commenting on the merit of the subject matter. Years later, the *New York Times* claimed the "stark, often grim black-and-white photographs revealed that Miss Welty's long-admired sense of observation was not limited to the ear, but extended to the eye as well" (3).

Despite the attention, Welty spent these years quietly, visiting with her friends whenever she had the chance. She was in no means a recluse, and in Jackson, she was a local celebrity. The town, proud of her accomplishments, held many celebratory events in her honor. Charlotte Capers, former director of the state's department of Archives and History, explained Welty's popularity:

> Jacksonians, along with Mississippians, have a terrible inferiority complex—they feel that everything in the world people say about them is bad and they have the feeling somehow that everything [Welty's] saying about Mississippi is good and funny and true. Where Faulkner didn't give a damn, and his writings were difficult, her personal popularity and the feeling of gratitude that she has represented us so well— we need this, and we're grateful for it. (*More Conversations* 4)

The Mississippi Arts Festival Week in May, 1973 was designated a Eudora Welty Celebration, and Governor William Waller officially declared Wednesday, May 2, Eudora Welty Day. A few days later Frank Hains, her friend and the arts editor of the *Jackson Daily News*, called and asked how she felt about the news. She was not sure what he was referring to, and he interrupted, "Do you mean, Eudora, that you don't know about the Pulitzer?" (*More Conversations* 3).

The Optimist's Daughter won the Pulitzer Prize, and Welty, gracious and modest, told reporters, "I'm just overwhelmed, dumbfounded and delighted. It is just like a dream. That sounds trite, but that's what it is. It just makes me want to work harder and harder" (*Conversations* 149).

In 1979 Welty was invited as an artist-in-residence at the British Studies Program at University College, Oxford. She enjoyed being in

England again, and as usual, she was dedicated and devoted to the program. She had students over for tea, and participated in the readings and sightseeing trips. Although she was shy, she was also quite visible, and the students enjoyed her company. While she was there, she asked one of the professors, William P. Cocke, where she could get her hair done. He made a few inquirers and she went the next day. When she returned, he asked her how it went and she said not very well: she didn't hear any gossip, she explained, which was the main reason for going to get her hair done.

That same year, Welty, a fan of President Jimmy Carter's, received the Presidential Medal of Freedom; President Carter presented it to her on the South Lawn of the White House. She also received the Medal for Literature from the American Book Awards, with a $15,000 cash prize. The next year, all of her previous story collections, in addition to the two Civil Rights stories "Where is the Voice Coming From" and "The Demonstrators," were published in *Collected Stories*. Welty said she wished should could have dropped a couple of stories from the collection, but the publishers persuaded her to leave them as they were. Some of the earliest stories were written in the days before she learned to revise, "I didn't know you *could* rewrite." (*More Conversations* 70). Although she privately revised some of the stories, she left them in their original form for the collection.

Welty's popularity blossomed, both in the critical and popular worlds. The paperback *Collected Stories* won the American Book Award, and *People* magazine named her one of the "25 Most Intriguing People of 1980." Although she didn't publish any other novels or stories, her work continued to appear in different forms. In 1974, Alfred Uhry and Robert Waldman adapted *The Robber Bridegroom*, turning into a successful musical that went on a nationwide tour. Although the musical differed in many ways from Welty's novel, she praised the adaptation. Then, in 1982, Alice Parker, a Juilliard-educated composer, turned Welty's novel *The Ponder Heart* into an opera. On opening night at the New Stage theatre in Jackson, newspapers from all over the country sent reporters to cover the event, and Jackson, as usual, presented the night as a gala for their adored citizen, Eudora Welty.

Privacy and Politics

Although she could now support herself mostly by her writing, Welty still gave many readings in the seventies and eighties. She was a popular entertainer, packing rooms full. Once she read at Stanford University and there were 1300 people packed in an auditorium that held a capacity of 600. Welty was a fantastic reader of her own work. One student explained, "What I found most interesting was the way this quiet, grandmotherly person was transformed into an actress and entertainer when she read some of her short stories" (qtd. in Waldron 319). She was also humorous and direct during the question and answer periods. One person asked her how Southerners could preserve oral tradition, and Welty replied, "Talk" (qtd. in Waldron 273). She usually read her early stories, choosing ones with dialogue and action. Once she forgot her glasses, and instead of saying anything, she merely read from memory: "I thought, I've read this story so many times that I don't need it. So, I had the book, I had it open. And I just went through it all from memory" (*More Conversations* 284).

Welty was just as gracious with her many interviews as she was with her readings, agreeing to hundreds over the course of her career. Nearly all of the interviewers seemed elated to speak with her, often comparing her to a sweet grandmother or a kind aunt. Reporters frequently tried to describe the sound of her soothing voice. A reporter for the *Jackson Daily* wrote: "Eudora Welty's voice is as Southern as the Delta is flat. It's bright, pleasant and precise. It sounds like pear honey tastes" (*Conversations* 342). Welty, too courteous to turn down requests, welcomed the reporters, and during the interviews she was "warm and humorously self-deprecating" (Krebs 7). By now she was gray and wrinkled, yet writers often pointed out her bright blue eyes and tall height. Novelist Anne Tyler noticed her "eyes are still as luminous as ever, radiating kindness and ... attention, you would have to call it; but attention of a special quality, with some gentle amusement accompanying it" (*More Conversations* 70). While many of the interview questions concerned specific stories or novels, reporters also wanted to know about Welty's writing habits and her politics.

Welty was always quite candid about her political leanings in interviews and her reasons for not bringing politics into her fiction. In the seventies, in particular, she was quite outspoken, and not all of her views were popular. For example, in an answer to a survey, she described the Women's Liberation as "Noisiness" (*Conversations* 36). Welty believed in equal rights, as in equal pay for men and women, for example; but she had never felt drawn to protests, and did not feel comfortable with the members of Women's Liberation as her "representatives."

She freely admitted she was a liberal Democrat, and that she was a huge fan of Adlai Stevenson's, and a foe of Nixon's politics. Once, in the seventies, she was kicked out of a Jackson restaurant because she was with two young men "with Jesus haircuts," and Welty quickly responded by writing a letter of complaint to the *Clarion-Ledger* (*Conversations* 65). As a citizen, she cared deeply about politics. But she was always clear about the line between literature and politics: "What is true is that I don't think of myself as a writer of fiction who seeks to make it a platform for my opinions ... I am a very interested citizen and try to keep informed on everything and to vote" (*Conversations* 226).

Welty felt hopeful about humanity, although admitted she was devastated by Kennedy's assassination: "I also loved John F. Kennedy; I thought something wonderful was going to happen in the world when he was elected. And that really vanished with his assassination" (*More Conversations* 114). She also admitted, later in her life, that she may have been naïve in her earlier sentiments about the civil rights movement— when she said that it was no more difficult for a novelist to enter the minds and hearts of the people than it ever had been before:

> I think I was mistaken in what you read about it being no harder than it ever was. I was sincere as far as I knew, but didn't know enough. It was harder. I think more effort had to be made, and that it was made, you know, as time went on. We had to learn to do it.... I guess we've been through an experience which was more profound than we'd guessed; both black and white.... Now, seeing how much more there was to communication than the wish, and the desire, and the heart, I feel have more to learn now than I had to learn then. (*Conversations*, 337)

Welty continued to place emphasis on the personal and specific relationships over the general, and what she saw change over the years in her home town gave her hope for the future: "I do feel that private relationships between blacks and whites have always been the steadying thing. I believe in private human relationships anyway, for under-standing. And I've always had faith that they would resolve problems. And I think by and large that that eventually has happened here in Jackson" (*More Conversations* 114).

Welty answered questions about fiction and politics, but most interviewers knew not to delve into Welty's personal life. Although she always spoke candidly, and often cooked the interviewer supper, or offered him or her bourbon, she refused to answer private questions about her friends, family, or herself. She would not agree to participate in a biography. Although Welty was certainly never a recluse like authors such as J.D. Salinger, she fiercely fended off private questions. The biography by Anne Waldron was actively discouraged by Welty, and she instructed her friends to also be taciturn in answering private questions about her life. Once when an interviewer asked her about how she would feel about a biography on herself, she replied:

> Shy, and discouraged at the very thought, because to me, a writer's work should be everything. A writer's whole feeling, the force of his whole life, can go into a story—but what he's worked for is to get an objective piece down on paper.... But your private life should be kept private. My own I don't think would particular interest anybody, for that matter. But I'd guard it; I feel strongly about that. They'd have a hard time trying to find something about me. I think I'd better burn everything up. It's best to burn letters, but at least I've never kept diaries or journals. (*Conversations* 81)

Welty believed passionately in guarding her privacy and allowing her fiction to stand on its own. She always stood by the fact that her characters were creations and not based on real people (except for the links between her mother and Becky in *The Optimist's Daughter*). She explained in her memoir, "I don't write by invasion into the life of a real person: my own sense of privacy is too strong for that; and I also know instinctively that living people to whom you are close—those known to you in ways too deep, too overflowing, ever to be plumbed outside love—do not yield to, could never fit into, the demands of the story" (109). She disliked people reading too much into her fiction, either overanalyzing or combing the pages for clues about her private life. She admitted her fiction was personal, not autobiographical, and "they aren't the same thing at all" (*Conversations* 214).

Welty felt comfortable behind the curtain of her "sheltered life," but she was not a naïve woman. She had dealt with much loss, and had taken strong stances on art and politics. Although a private person, she knew when to speak out. For example, in 1975, Frank Hains was found murdered in Jackson—he was naked, his hands and feet bound with neckties, and his mouth gagged. When a man with a record of arrests for rape and murder was charged, gossip about Hains's "lifestyle" became rampant in Jackson. Welty quickly silenced the gossip by paying tribute to Hains; she wrote an editorial for his column in the *Jackson Daily News*, praising him and his work, and her words seemed to have a reassuring effect on the community (Waldron 321). Furthermore, although Welty reminisced about her happy childhood in Jackson, she also recognized the more hateful and violent histories of the city, and she was glad for the changes in racial attitudes: "Thank God things did change a lot in the South ... Jackson itself has changed incredibly, just accelerated itself into trying to become more civilized" (*More Conversations* 237).

Some scholars believe that this emphasis on her sheltered life and her congenial personality dissuaded critics from taking her work seriously. Feminists critics, for example, avoided her work until recently, especially after Welty made several dismissive remarks about feminism in the early seventies. Scholar Carol Ann Johnston remarks, "Because of critical underevaluation, the literary establishment has not until very recently granted Welty the place that she deserves as one of America's greatest writers" (4). Her reputation as a regionalist and the critics' perception of her as writer who ignored social-political themes, possibly explained why she failed to receive a Nobel Prize. One of her admirers, Reynolds Price, wrote that selective attention to her work "has resulted in a partial, even distorted sense of Welty as the mild, sonorous, 'affirmative' kind of artist" (Johnston 178).

More recent criticism has challenged that view of her as a simple, modest writer, and instead examined the complexity of her work; however, early in her career, Welty was often categorized as a regional writer. She dismissed the neat label: "I just think of myself as writing about human beings and I happen to live in a region, as do we all, so I write what I know—it's the same case for any writer living anywhere. I also happen to love my particular region. If this shows, I don't mind" (*Conversations* 87). Most critics now point out that her work surpasses a particular region, and Johnston even goes as far to say that Welty "has located her work in a tradition of British and continental writers, more so than in the continuum of American fiction" (xi). It was true that Welty most often wrote about the South, however, unlike Faulkner, she did not feel especially encumbered by the history of the region, and simply wrote about the people around her. And yet *like* Faulkner, her work transcends region and presents a universal appeal.

A BOURBON AND WATER

Although throughout her career, Welty dissuaded glimpses into her personal life, in 1983, when Welty was invited to Harvard to give three lectures to graduate students, she spoke of personal childhood memories. She was now seventy-four years old. She wrote three new lectures for the program: "Listening," "Learning to See," and "Finding a Voice." These three lectures documented her childhood and its various influences on her as a writer. Swelling crowds showed up to hear her speak. A year later, Harvard University Press published the three lectures in a book called *One Writer's Beginnings*. The book, to Welty's surprise, received extravagant reviews. It stayed on the *New York Times* best seller list for almost a year, and was named one of the top ten books of 1984 by *USA Today*.

The book was popular with both critics and readers, although a few critics found the glowing picture of her family "too good to be true" (Waldron 330). The book, a reflection on the sensory memories of her early years, portrays her family with complete adoration, and in typical fashion, Welty does not address politics, culture, or social issues. However, this quiet memoir also reveals something about Welty's inner-strength, suggests Waldron: "By many standards, Eudora Welty's life has been a long ordeal of personal loss, grief, hard work, and loneliness. The fact that she does not see it this way adds to her glory" (332).

By the mid-eighties, Welty was settling into old age, although she said, "I forget I'm this old. I notice it in lots of ways, but the only bad part is the death of friends, people I've known fifty ears and am used to seeing all the time ... That's the worst" (*More Conversations* 142). A reporter marveled at her health: "Her memory is remarkable, and her conversation is precise and alive with the wonder of discovery" (*More Conversations* 76). Her blue eyes still shone brightly, but she walked slowly, hunched over and using a cane. Although her vision was still good, she was starting to lose her hearing, which discouraged her. She always loved eavesdropping; many quirky lines that she had overheard would then appear in a story. She said for a writer, ears were just as important as eyes: "Your ears should be like magnets. I used to be able to hear people in back and in front of me and on the street. I don't hear as much as I used to. It's so *maddening* not to overhear remarks" (*More Conversations* 86).

For most of her life, when she was writing, she worked in the mornings and reserved the evenings for her friends. Welty, who considered herself by nature a short-story writer and not a novelist, often said she could write anywhere, that she only needed privacy, "And sometimes the only way to get privacy is to leave home" (*Conversations* 345). She always enjoyed the act of writing, even though it was difficult. Sometimes she even laughed aloud as she wrote. As she aged and her fame grew, she had less time to write. Then in 1988, the arthritis in her hands prevented her from typing and she had to write in longhand; dictation did not work for her. When she was asked what her ideal work day would look like, if she did not have any other obligations or physical discomforts, she said she would wake up early and write the entire day without interruptions: "And at the end of the day, about five or six o'clock, I'd stop for good that day. And I'd have a drink, a bourbon and water, watch the evening news—'MacNeil-Lehrer News Hour'—and then I could do anything I wanted to do" (*More Conversations* 172).

She seemed grateful for all of her support, and showed no major regrets about her life. When asked about marriage, she said it never came up, but that she would not have been opposed to the idea: "I like love and affection and friendship—it just never did work out that it'd happen. But I would have been very glad if it had" (*More Conversations* 142).

The house on Pinehurst had not changed much over the years, except now nearly every flat surface was covered in books or papers. Welty never used an air-conditioner, but the house, to visitors, felt breezy and open, even in the Mississippi heat. The old oak tree, which her mother had never allowed to be cut down, still stood, towering over the yard. Although the house had not changed, its surroundings had. Now

Pinehurst Street was heavy with traffic. Jackson's population had swelled to over 300,000. One interviewer aptly described the changes: "The grand homes that once graced State Street have given way to Cooke's Prosthetics and Cash-in-a-Flash Pawn Shop" (*More Conversations* 80).

The changes in Jackson, however, did not alter the capital's adoring attitude toward Welty. She was a beloved local celebrity, with the *Jackson Daily News* covering her every move. For example, when she traded in her old upright Royal typewriter for an electric model, the story made headlines. Welty never complained about the attention: "Jackson is very understanding of me. I'm very proud of it—my relationship with my hometown" (*Conversations* 258). Jackson showered her with honors and celebrations, such as when the town turned out to celebrate her 75th birthday. The Mississippi Department of Archives and History began a year long program in encouraging the appreciation of Welty's work, and Welty deeded her home to the Department, allowing her to live there without paying taxes. The home of her birthplace, on North Congress Street, was turned into a writers' center. When the city library moved into the remodeled Sears, Roebuck building, it was renamed the Eudora Welty Library, opening with another hometown celebration of Eudora. Welty, who loved a good story, told Elizabeth Bennett that people in Jackson began to think she lived there, saying, "You're the lady that lives at the *Liberry*" (*More Conversations* 214).

Welty felt grateful for Jackson's attention and devotion; however, by the time her 80th birthday came around, she wondered if she could handle yet another celebration: "In Jackson, since I've lived here all my life, everybody just loves to celebrate things with me. They're very sweet about it. But I don't know if I could stand to have that celebrated. It's too much" (*More Conversations* 182). However, true to form, on her 80th birthday, the Jackson Symphony Orchestra performed two new works dedicated to Welty, and then the audience sang "Happy Birthday" and gave her a standing ovation. Waldron attests to the magnitude of Welty's fame: "By this time Eudora had been sanctified, canonized, apotheosized in Jackson, the town where she had ridden her bicycle around the rotund of the state capital, where she had made friends, if not conquests, in high school, where she had first begun to write, and where she had written nearly all of her work. The town had nurtured her and now it rewarded her" (340).

Her honors were not only local, but also national and international. Some of these awards and honors included the National Medal of Arts (1986); the Chevalier de L'ordre d'Arts et Lettres medal (France, 1987); and the Mississippi Institute of Arts and Letters Lifetime Achievement Award (1988). In 1991, she received the Peggy V. Helmerich Distinguished Author Award ($20,000); the National Book Foundation's Medal for Distinguished Contribution to American Letters ($10,000); and the Rea Ward for the Short Story ($25,000). In addition to these honors, her portrait was added to the National Portrait Gallery of the Smithsonian Institution, and she was given an honorary doctorate from Princeton University.

FINAL YEARS

In 1992, Welty was asked if she would have any more books coming out. "You never know—I don't know," she said. "I love to write. I'll never stop that, never stop loving to write. So we shall see" (*More Conversations* 242). Although she did not publish any new fiction after *The Optimist's Daughter*, more of her early photographs were published by the University Press of Mississippi, and she also collaborated with Ronald A. Sharpe to edit *The Norton Book for Friendship*.

Welty gave hundreds of interviews, and after the success of *One Writer's Beginnings*, thousands more wanted to interview her. However, now overwhelmed by all of the attention, she turned most of them down. One of the last interviews with Welty, in 1994, describes her failing health and tremendous perseverance. "At age 85, the writer Eudora Welty is a fine old tree, bent and knotted but sagely alive. A fractured spine gives her posture a parenthetical curve. She worked with a pronounced stoop, very slowly, navigating even the broadest floor like a tightrope. Touched by a Delta drawl, her voice is faint but deliberate" (*More Conversations* 289). At this point, she was battling with cataracts and arthritis, and her writing days were over. But she still read every night before bed and in the morning, and continued to spend time with friends and family. She also maintained her sharp sense of humor, and assured reporters that she still had ideas and things she wanted to say.

She was still very much a celebrity in Jackson. Although she ate at local restaurants and tried to accommodate the occasional interview, she also found it necessary to take actions in guarding her privacy: "Welty's success has made her an unwitting tourist attraction. Fans often arrive on the porch seeking an audience or an autograph—so many that the typically gracious Welty has had to put a 'Do Not Disturb" sign (*More Conversations* 293).

Eudora Welty, one of the most revered figures in contemporary American letters, received nearly every major award bestowed upon the great American writers. In 1992 she was awarded the Frankel Prize by the National Endowment for the Humanities, and a year later received the PEN/Malmud Award. In 1996 she was inducted into France's Legion of Honor. She was also the first living writer to ever be included in the prestigious Library of America series of collected works by America's greatest writers, which include Walt Whitman, Mark Twain, Henry James, and William Faulkner, among others.

Once Welty was asked if her life was lonely. She replied, "No. I feel in touch. I like doing things, you know, privately. But I like to write with a window that looks out on to the street.... I like to be a part of my world. No, writing is solitary. But I don't feel lonely" (*More Conversations* 153). Miss Eudora Welty died in Jackson on July 23, 2001. She was ninety-two years old.

WORKS CITED

Johnston, Carol Ann. *Eudora Welty: A Study of Short Fiction*. New York: Twayne Publishers, 1997.

Krebs, Albin. "Author Eudora Welty Dies at 92." *New York Times on the Web*. 23 July 2001. <http://www.nytimes.com/2001/97/23/arts/23CND-WELTY.html>.

Porter, Katherine Anne. "Introduction." Johnston. In *Eudora Welty: A Study of Short Fiction*. New York: Twayne Publishers, 1997: 151–157.

Prenshaw, Peggy Whitman, ed. *Conversations with Eudora Welty*. Jackson: University Press of Mississippi, 1984.

———.*More Conversations with Eudora Welty*. Jackson: University Press of Mississippi, 1996.

Price, Reynolds. "Review." In *Eudora Welty: A Study of Short Fiction*. New York: Twayne Publishers, 1997:. 173–178.

Trilling, Diana. "Fiction in Review." In *Critical Essays on Eudora Welty*. Boston: G.K. Hall & Co. 1989: 39–42.

Trilling, Lionel. "American Fairy Tale." In *Critical Essays on Eudora Welty*. Boston: G.K. Hall & Co. 1989 31–32.

Turner, W. Craig and Lee Emling Harding, eds. *Critical Essays on Eudora Welty.* Boston: G.K. Hall & Co., 1989.

Vande Kieft, Ruth M. *Eudora Welty.* Boston: Twayne Publishers, 1987.

Warren, Robert Penn. "The Love and the Separateness in Miss Welty." In *Critical Essays on Eudora Welty.* Boston: G.K. Hall & Co. 1989: 42–51.

Welty, Eudora. *One Writer's Beginnings.* Cambridge, MA: Warner Books, 1983.

————. "Must the Novelist Crusade?" *Stories, Essays, and Memoir.* New York: The Library of America, 1998. 803–814.

Waldron, Ann. *Eudora: A Writer's Life.* New York: Anchor Books, 1998.

SAMUEL ARKIN

Eudora Welty's Fictional Childhood: A Craving Born of Suspense

"The events in our lives happen in a sequence in time, but in their significance to ourselves they find their own order, a timetable not necessarily—perhaps not possibly— chronological. The time as we know it subjectively is often the chronology that stories and novels follow: it is the continuous thread of revelation."

(Kreyling and Ford, eds., 914)

"Living is being in transit." (948)

Fiction takes the accidental occurrences of a life and gives them meaning, by sorting out the difference between the way they are aligned, and the way that we align them. Determining this difference demands an active place of memory, where time itself can become a subject. The activity of a life is bound by the constraints of time and place, and for Welty, the task of autobiography is figuring out whether the place that feels like home has made time feel like time. Necessity is created by art to the extent that it is art that gives us our sense of time, as we know it. We share a sense of place with others; it is time that is personal. The concept of travel, or of the story, stands for the confluence of time and place in the act of memory: "The memory is a living thing—it too is in transit" (948). Welty's sense of perspective is similar to her sense of the meaning of travel. When stationary, origin and destination both feel like a remembered dream. The accidents of time can be called random only from the mooring of a certain place. For Eudora Welty, this fiction is a principle that extends out of art and becomes an ethics, marking what is daringly imaginative in her own work: "I am a writer who came of a sheltered life. A sheltered life can be a daring life as well. For all serious daring starts from within" (948). As she wrote towards the end of her career, "all facts are a verdict". This is not a conclusion that can be reached without the judgment of fiction.

Sympathy is cultivated by storytelling, and may start with self-sympathy, or a sense of one's own origin. For Welty, this means being able to give an account of where one comes from. Welty was born in Jackson, Mississippi, and it remained her primary home in a life of near constant travel. Welty could have stayed and gone to college in Jackson, but her desire to travel brought her to Mississippi State College for Women, and then to the University of Wisconsin, where she discovered Yeats' "Song of Wandering Aengus", which haunts her book of stories "The Golden Apples". It was in Wisconsin that she started to believe in her passion for writing, and her mother responded in kind, her father by the gift of a dictionary. In Welty's life it is very difficult to separate fiction into fact, which does not mean that her story is false. The facts of her life are the act of telling a life, and it is the telling that makes the use of the word "act" possible. This too is a fear born out of autobiography—her father was a lover of fact in a manner that wanted to excluded fiction. He was a man who believed in monuments, and the assurance with which he put forth his vision is in turn monumentalized in Welty's work.

When a new building was being constructed for the Lamar Life insurance company in Jackson in 1925, Welty's father took the family to observe the workman's progress at every step of the process. When completed, he gave a little speech that Welty records: "Not a dollar was borrowed nor a security sold for the erection of this new building, and it is all paid for. The building will stand, now and always, free from all debt, as a most valuable asset to policy-holders" (927). The building, as belonging to an insurance company, is a perfect image of her father's sensibility. It is a kind of impossibility, an insurance building that did not need to prey on people's hope, in the form of investments, in order to be built. Life insurance, in fact, does need to profit from people's expectations of the future, an emotion that we cannot call hope because to do so would be to counterfeit the reality of death. Nonetheless, Welty's father imagines a free monument that is for the policy-holders, an act made possible by the fact that he both worked in the building and was treated like a policy-holder there—one of his son's became an architect, the other an insurance salesman. Welty herself worked in the bottom of the building during the great depression, in Mississippi's first radio station. Welty's image of her father's occupation is her father's vision of memory, a memory that he insured would survive according to the optimism of what Welty calls his "imaginative conception" (927).

In any given life, certain roles are thrust upon us, and for Eudora Welty, there is a way of hearing one's role that is the mark of what she calls the storyteller. This process occurs in time, but is also a manner of telling time: "Learning stamps you with its moments. Childhood's learning is made up of movements. It isn't steady. It's a pulse". The pulse is a process of hearing, and the relationship between hearing and seeing is a metaphor, for Welty, for the relationship between feeling and thinking. She argues that if we hear time, we might begin to see (or have revealed to us) what it is to distinguish between what is "steady" and what is "pulsing". We think of a pulse as being regular, even steady, but Welty teaches us, and was taught by her own story, to hear and feel what is irregular. This is the primary occupation of her fiction. Welty reveals from within the rhythms of ordinary speech, of gossip, what is curious and worthy of something beyond pity.

The quote above is taken from her memoir, "One Writer's Beginnings". In that memoir, Welty describes the process of learning that she believes accounts for her own capacity as a writer of fiction. Stories follow a time that Welty asserts is not strictly chronological, like the movement of letters through the post or the ebb and flow of one's attention during an extended period of travel—for example, a description of a voyage by train with her father: "Side by side and separately, we each lost ourselves in the experience of not missing anything, of seeing everything, of knowing each time what the blows of the whistle meant" (915). Human events are impossibly outside of time—that is what gives and takes away their meaning, what makes them not possible, necessarily. In fiction, Welty takes "the time as we know it subjectively" and makes it the continuous thread of revelation.

Stories and lives depend upon what one's sense of a fact is. For Welty, there are the facts of life and the facts of a life. Personal history is a bit like gossip's relation to the truth—the one is always a disclosure of the other. Welty's anecdotes about her childhood accommodate the perspectives of all involved, so that an error pointed out to her by another when she was young has become her own scene of recognition, an act that does not occur at the expense of the other people involved. For Welty, an imaginative mistaking of a fact, whether natural or personal, is not always strictly a lie, and is usually a compromise:

> The word "moon" came into my mouth as though fed to me out of a silver spoon. Held in my mouth the moon became a word. It had the roundness of a Concord grape Grandpa took off his vine and gave me to suck out of its skin and swallow whole, in Ohio. This love did not prevent me from living for years in foolish error about the moon. The new moon just appearing in the west was the rising moon to me. The new should be rising. And in early childhood the sun and moon, those opposite reigning powers, I just as easily assumed rose in east and west respectively in their opposite sides of the sky, and like partners in a reel they advanced, sun from the east, moon from the West, crossed over (when I wasn't looking) and went down on the other side. My father couldn't have know I believed that when, bending behind me and guiding my shoulder, he positioned me at our telescope in the front yard and, with careful adjustment of the focus, brought moon close to me. (848)

The confusion of word and moon is an imaginative process, and as such deserves fictional recognition. As a word, the moon can be held in the mouth, and emerge as a part of personal memory. Welty's love is for the word moon, and the natural thing is a result to be determined by the instrument of perception. For Welty, this instrument is a combination of familial and personal history, blended in a way to make the naturalness of the story replace the potential unnaturalness of the relation between moon and grape. Welty's subjective feelings are an image that is shared by her family—the moon is as personal and as distant as her memory of a time with her Grandfather in Ohio. One's love of association seems to grow into a love and a reverence for place. The process makes one's connection to places exactly as arbitrary as the development of one's imagination—in this case, origin is both retained and confused.

The natural world has its inherited exigencies, but so too does the imaginative: "The new should be rising". This use of "should" speaks of necessity as a relation between the imaginative and the actual—a difference that can only be appreciated in the act of retelling one's past. There is a similar use of the word "couldn't": "My father couldn't have known I believed in that ..." Here, the father's rational inability is touched with sympathy and a kind of regret by Welty, as his failure, either of communication or of imagination, is part of a gesture that is an attempt to communicate something wondrous. The comparison is between a literally mistaken perception and an accurate scientific one, and the adequacy of the latter is revealed to be only partial. Instead, Welty comes away with a profound and lasting impression of the interchangeability of moon and sun, those "opposite reigning powers" that have so long governed the imaginative cosmos:

> This type of mistake is contrasted with a mendacity that is not strictly a lie. In the Welty household, as she tells us with a more or less straight face, "there wasn't any lying" (854): It was taken entirely for granted that there wasn't any lying in our family, and I was advanced in adolescence before I realized that in plenty of homes where I played with schoolmates and went to their parties, children lied to their parents and parents lied to their children and to each other. It took me a long time to realize that these very same everyday lies, and the stratagems and jokes and tricks and dares that went with them, were in fact the basis of the scenes I so well loved to hear about and hoped for and treasured in the conversation of adults. My instinct—the dramatic instinct—was to lead me, eventually, on the right track for a storyteller: the scene was full of hints, pointers, suggestions, and promises of things to find out and know about human beings. I had to grow up and learn to listen for the unspoken as well as the spoken—and to know a truth, I also had to recognize a lie. (854)

The reason that this lie is beyond being responsible to the truth is in the telling, and the relation between the original telling and a later dramatic retelling. Welty was surrounded by stories as a child, and she listened to them in a particular way. Welty's was a pulsating, mobile listening, and her use of the word "dramatic" stands for this—in itself, the "everyday lie" is the very definition of what is mundane and almost unthinking. It is only as part of a scene that the everyday strategy of the lie becomes a "promise of things to find out and know about human beings". As Welty explains it: "Years later, beginning with my story 'Why I live at the P.O.', I wrote reasonably often in the form of a monologue that takes possession of the speaker. How much more gets told besides!" (853). The quotidian lie that is the rehearsal of a habitual scene becomes dramatic when you can hear the unspoken. This unspoken is the recognition that comes when one understands what is dramatic about the possession of the speaker by the story.

As Welty has told us, there was no lying in her home—as an act of autobiography, she is almost teasing us, daring us to accuse her of lying here. There was, however, the felicitous avoidance of the truth, which amounts, through the process of storytelling, to the meaningful recognition of a lie:

> The sudden silence in the double bed meant my younger brothers had both keeled over in sleep, and I in the single bed at my end of the porch would be lying electrified, waiting for this to be the night when she'd tell me what she'd promised for so long. Just as she bent to kiss me I grabbed her and asked: "Where do babies come from?" My poor mother! But something saved her every time. Almost any night I put the baby question to her, suddenly, as if the whole outdoors exploded, Professor Holt would start to sing. The Holt's lived next door; he taught penmanship (the Palmer method), typing, bookkeeping and shorthand at the night school. "Dear, this isn't a very good time for you to hear mother, is it?" (855)

We have a sense, through Welty's staging of the scene, of the regularity of the exchange, as the opportunity for a promised story is finally at hand. This is how the time was measured for Welty as a child. She was a prodigious reader, and her practice of reading gave her a way of living: "Ever since I was first read to, then started reading to myself, there has never been a line read that I didn't hear. As my eyes followed the sentence, a voice was saying it silently to me. It isn't my mother's voice, or the voice of any person I can identify, certainly not my own. It is human, but inward, and it is inwardly that I listen to it. It is to me the voice of the story or the poem itself" (851). Her mother's story telling continues:

> She told'd me that the mother and father had to both want the baby. This couldn't be enough. I knew she was not trying to fib to me, for she never did fib, but also I could not help but know she was not really telling me. And more than, I was afraid of what I was going to hear next. This was partly because she wanted to tell me in the dark. I though she might be afraid. In something like childish hopelessness I thought she probably couldn't tell, just as she couldn't lie. (855)

This use of couldn't is very much like the one Welty uses to describe her father's use of the telescope: "My Father couldn't have know I believed that ..." (848). What is important is the relationship Welty is able to achieve, a relationship with her own telling of the story, as she narrates the story she told herself as a child in the form of a memoir meant to describe her origins as a writer. The relation between fact and fiction, in this case the facts of life and the life of fiction, is best expressed as an adults description of her own childlike disappointment at the way her mother told her a true story. Her mother has been asked by the young Welty to tell a story that involves facts, and the avoidance of the truth of those facts is retold by Welty. In both cases, in the Mother's initial telling and Welty's subsequent re-telling, the common register of truth is in the telling. The "hopelessness" that Welty felt at the time, re-accounted for and called something like "childish", is not either the child's longing or the mother's telling, it is the relationship between them. This relationship goes both ways:

> On the night we came closest to having it over with, she started to tell me without being asked, and I ruined it by yelling, "Mother, look at the lightning bugs!" (855)

The young child who asked to hear the story in bed each night, lying "electrified" with hope, now points excitedly to an electricity that is outside. The mother is not guilty of not telling the story, and she is acquitted by Welty's sense of what it means to have heard the drama of the telling of the story. Welty understands her mother's situation as a kind of double negative, or at least this is how she retells her childlike understanding—her mother both "couldn't tell", and "couldn't lie". This double meaning is what it is to know a truth through the recognition of what lying is. It is Welty's fictional method.

Soon after telling us about his episode, Welty contrasts it with another story her mother told her: "Not being able to bring herself to open that door to reveal its secret, one of those days, she opened another door" (856). The difference between the stories is the difference between what is secret to all people and what a private secret might be. While playing in her Mother's room, Welty is given permission to use a lock of her mother's hair as a plaything. The lock of hair is kept in one of her Mother's "treasure boxes", and one day when she goes to look for it Eudora finds "a small white cardboard box such as her engraved calling cards came in from the printing house. It was tightly closed, but I opened it, to find to my puzzlement and covetousness two polished buffalo nickels, embedded in white cotton" (856):

> I rushed with this open box to my mother and asked if I could run out and spend the nickels. "No!" She exclaimed in a most passionate way. She seized the box into her own hands. I begged her; somehow I had started to cry. Then she sat down, drew me to her, and told me that I had had a little brother who had come before I did, and who had died as a baby before I was born. And these two nickels that I'd wanted to claim as my find were his. They had lain on his eyelids, for a purpose untold and unimaginable. "He was a fine little baby, my first baby, and he shouldn't have died. But he did. It was because your mother almost died at the same time," she told me. "In looking after me, they too nearly forgot about the little baby." She told me the wrong secret—not how babies could come but how they could Die, how they could be forgotten about. (856)

The moral of the stories is not something to be taken from either one individually: "The future story writer in the child I was must have taken unconscious note and stored it away then: one secret is liable to be revealed in the place of another that is harder to tell, and the substitute secret when nakedly exposed is often the more appalling" (857). The discovery of the two coins is the occasion for her mother to tell a memory. The story is like the coins themselves, practically untold and unimaginable. Memory is a giving thing whose gifts, always revealed in a steady order that has been forgotten, are never predictable.

Welty was diagnosed as a young child with a condition the doctor's called "fast-beating heart", for which they prescribed rest. For Welty, this meant being prescribed a kind of "suspense", where time was observed or heard rather than strictly felt. The bed where she was confined happened to be right across from her school, and so instead of going to school Welty heard the sounds of other children at school. She was "homesick" for school, and so the act of learning was not an enlightenment, but a relation to nostalgia. While her mother occasionally gave her lessons in Arithmetic, her bed was covered with story books, and real school was something to be illuminated like Princess Labam lighted her city from the rooftop of her palace.

Her parents kept her company in the evenings, by fitting a newspaper to a lampshade so that Eudora could sleep and they could read the evening papers and talk without disturbing her:

> My parents draped the lampshade with a sheet of the daily paper, which was tilted, like a hatbrim, so that they could sit in their rockers in a lighted part of the room and I could supposedly go to sleep in the protected dark of the bed. They sat talking. What was thus dramatically made a present of to me was the secure sense of the hidden observer. As long as I could make myself keep awake, I was free to listen to every word my parents said between them. I don't remember that any secrets were revealed to me. But I was present in the room with the chief secret there was—the two of them, father and mother, sitting there as one. I was conscious of this secret and of my fast-beating heart in step together. (862)

For Welty, this autobiographical fact is of importance for the fiction of her future: "A conscious act grew out of this by the time I began to write stories: getting my distance, a prerequisite of my understanding of human events, is the way I begin work" (862). It occurs also in relation to the past, as this is a practice that she shared, in part, with her Mother. At her Grandmother's house, Eudora's mother says "And here's where I first began to read my Dickens," pointing. "Under that very bed. Hiding my candle. To keep them from knowing what I was up to all night" (888).

For Welty, writing an autobiography, there is a difference between what she knew then and what she knows now. This gap articulates the difference between the perspective of a narrator, and the perspective of the events being narrated in real time. What is of interest in "One Writer's Beginnings" is that Welty is both of these things, whereas in her stories she is writing about others, real and imagined. This is not simply a matter of happenstance: for Welty, the perspective she is bringing to life in "One Writer's Beginnings" is an image for what she thinks is of lasting value for the reading and writing of fiction. As she says about her love of books, "I knew this was bliss, I knew it at the time". This is one of the few times in the memoir that Welty states explicitly that she knew or felt something at the time, with the implication that it is not something that she has gained with the hindsight afforded by the work of personal literary remembrance. For Welty, there is something meaningful in the ability to love stories: "I remember Mother reading the new issue of Time magazine while taking the part of the Wolf in a game of "Little Red Riding Hood" with the children. She'd just look up at the right time, long enough to answer—in character—"The better to eat you with, my dear," and go back to her place in the war news. For Welty, her Mother's transition between the two spheres is, perhaps, a transition between genre accomplished across generations, and a kind of communication and parental love that is to be valued.

STORIES

Welty's concern with acting, and with the difference between a secret and a lie are preoccupations that run throughout an early story, "Lily Daw and the Three Ladies". The scene is set in a post office, where two of the ladies receive the news that another woman, named Lily, has been accepted at an "Institute for the Feeble Minded" called Ellisville. This is civilization's acceptance of the mad. Their reaction occurs in an emotional register where the acting involved in decorum is heard differently. The women take pleasure in telling stories about Lily's own social misadventures, and the act of storytelling is foregrounded throughout. The comparison, between the ladies own lives and their retelling of what they perceive about Lily's life is crucial: "Oh, she (Lily) can be a lady— she can be," said Mrs. Carson, shaking her head and turning her eyes up. "That's just what breaks your heart" (6).

> The women have seen Lily at a show the previous evening, and her behavior there has become all the proof the women need in order to feel justified sending her away. Aside from the formality of the occasion, and the fact that Lily is taken advantage of for profit by a ticket vendor, Lily's only crime seems to be taking reasonable behavior too far—"And Lily acted so nice. She was a perfect lady— just set in her seat and stared" (6). The women imagine that Lily's focus is empty, even as their focus during the show is clearly not on the music, but rather on what Lily is focusing on: "The point is, what did she do after the show?" asked Mrs. Watts practically. "Lily has gotten so she is very mature for her age." "Oh, Etta!" Protested Mrs. Carson, looking at her wildly for a moment. "And that's how come we are sending her to Ellisville," finished Mrs. Watts. (6)

Why are the women sending Lily to Ellisville? Their own idea as to what she might have possibly done, their reaction to that possibility, has replaced any actual report of Lily's activity. Mrs. Watts' question is never literally answered, it is left hanging in a manner that suggests the unspeakable breach of decorum the women collectively imagine, with Mrs. Carson's wild look standing for the proper reflection of madness by civilization—we are not sure whether she exclaims out of sympathy for Mrs. Watts' position, or for Lily's. The reason for sending Lily to Ellisville is a question, but a question that must be asked and never answered out of necessity.

Lily's relation to the three ladies is orchestrated through social events where acting of various kinds is required. First the show, and then a marriage:

> "To find Lily is a different thing," said Aimee Slocum. "Where in the wide word do suppose she'd be?" It was Mrs. Watts who was carrying the letter. "I don't see a sign of her

84

either on this side of the street or on the other side," Mrs.
Carson declared as they walked along. Ed Newton was
stringing Redbird school tablets on the wire across the store.
"If you're after Lily, she come in here while ago and told me
she was fixin' to git married," he said. "Ed Newton!" cried
the ladies all together, clutching one another. Mrs Watts
began to fan herself at once with the letter from Ellisville.
She wore widow's black, and the least thing made her hot. (6)

Looking for Lily is figured as a kind of pursuit—we hear this in the use
of the word "after" as Welty uses it in the mouth of Ed Newton—it
could describe the pursuit of a concerned friend after someone who has
gone missing, or of a sheriff after a criminal. There is relief in sending
Lily to Ellisville, literally represented by the fan made out of the letter
with which Mrs. Watts cools herself, that is difficult to explain. The
difficulty is in understanding the difference between the avoidance of
personal discomfort, and just action for another person. Who are the
women in the story acting for, themselves or for Lily? Do the women
actively not want Lily to have the chance to participate in social things?
If she is slow, and cannot understand what she is doing, then why do they
need to save her from herself? The image Welty creates with Lily is of a
person going through the social motions without apparent
disturbance—this person is described by other people, and it is this act
of description that is a figure for a human relation, and vice versa. The
women's charity is also a failure of observation, and self reflection: "Why
she is not. She's going to Ellisville, Ed," said Mrs. Carson gently. "Mrs.
Watts and I and Aimee Slocum are paying her way out of our own
pockets. Besides, the boys of Victory are on their honor. Lily's not going
to get married, that's just an idea she's got in her head" (7).

The story partly takes the form of the female exchange of story—
like the gossip that was a fixture of Welty's youth. Women are
exchanging information, but the civility this exchange affords occurs at
the expense of a scapegoat. The women talk, unthinkingly, and the
degree of consciousness with which they pursue their goal is one of
Welty's central questions, a question that she answers by writing stories.
The women are willing to share their language to a certain extent with
Lily: "What we've got to do is persuade Lily it will be nicer to go to
Ellisville" (7). To say that they must persuade her is to acknowledge a

degree of reasonableness in Lily, while simultaneously betraying a failure of reason and sympathy both in themselves. The women have themselves been unknowingly persuaded by a set of inherited social practices, and their practice of them is acting without conscience. This is different from Lily's unreflective action, although the two serve as foils for one another. Lily's crime, as one of the women says, is that she "never understood anything" (7). It is difficult to tell, however, what understanding is—isn't understanding simply doing what society offers perfectly? Is the women's gossipy persecution of Lily a greater understanding of societies rituals? The differentiating factor is in neither the women nor Lily, but the way they are both a part of Welty's story.

The women do eventually catch up with Lily. They find her in a house, and briefly retell the story of Lily's life, a life fractured by the early death of a mother and violence, even scarring, at the hands of an abusive and possibly mad father. When they do find her, they interrogate her in a tone that could be either that of a lawyer or a concerned provider. Lily is going to get married, she tells them, to a musician from the show she saw last night. Immediately, the women subject her to another of their fantasies: "Did he—did he do anything to you?" In the long run, it was still only Mrs. Watts who could take charge. "Oh yes'm," said Lilly" (9). Earlier, Lily herself shows self-consciousness, in that she diagnosis the other women with envy: "Going to get married", she says, "and I bet you wish you was me now" (9).

> The women are increasingly revealed to be not simply passive recipients of cultures bounty, but active agents, even legal prosecutors in the name of a decorum they believe in. The women don't simply want to know if the man did anything to Lily, they must know what he did: "What?" demanded Aimee Slocum, rising up and tottering before her scream. "What?" she called out in the hall. "Don't ask her what," said Mrs. Carson, coming up behind. "Tell me, Lily —just yes or no—are you the same as you were?" "He had a red coat," said Lily graciously. "He took little sticks and went ping-pong! Ding-dong!" "Oh, I think I'm going to faint," said Aimee Slocum, but they said, "No, you're not." "The xylophone!" cried Mrs. Watts. "The xylophone player! Why,

the coward, he ought to be run out of town on a rail!" "Out of town? He is out of town, by now," cried Aimee. "All right! We'll bring him back!" cried Mrs. Watts. "He can't get away from me!" (10)

Lily is excited about her impending marriage, and the women offer her a series of corrupt bargains in exchange for her agreeing to go to Ellisville. When then find her in the house, Lily is preparing a "hope chest", in which she has placed soap and towels. The women tell her the things they will give her to put into the chest if she agrees to go to Ellisville, a cruel exchange seeing as in so doing they take away the object of her hope, replacing it with theirs. One of the women offers Lily "a pretty little Bible with your name on it in real gold" (11). Welty's mother often told of how her father offered her an entire set of Dickens if she would agree to cut her hair—it was believed that long hair was unhealthy for women. This was forgivable—a false prejudice believed in out of care— somehow the care that the ladies offer is almost completely corrupted. The women claim to have consulted an even greater authority than prejudice, God, and continue to try and convince Lily. Finally, Lily asks if she can take her hope chest to Ellisville, and the women say she can. She is won over: "Lily lookup up at them, and her eyes gleamed. She cocked her head and spoke out in a proud imitation of someone—someone utterly unknown. "O.K.—Toots!"

As if prophetically, Lily has put forth the sound of the train the women have already booked for her to go to Ellisville. The entire town is assembled to see "Lily all dressed up", and a band has assembled spontaneously, "without any orders" (12). The women are continuing to help Lily—they sneak her on the train, and are going to "help Lily change trains and be sure she went in the right direction" (12). The crime is that helping Lily is the same thing as helping themselves. Lily is boxed in between two of the women on the train, a beautiful hat she purchased earlier having been taken from her: "Lily sat between them on the plush seat with her hair combed and pinned up into a know under a small blue hat which was Jewel's exchange for the pretty one" (12). People always seem to be helping Lily look appropriately. The story begins in a post office, and as is common with Welty, the form of the letter and the voyage are intertwined:

Aimee Slocum had been getting the outgoing mail stamped and bundled. She stood In the aisle of the coach now, tears shaking from her eyes. "Good-by, Lily," she said. She was the one who felt things "Good-by, silly," said Lily. "Oh, dear, I hope they get our telegram to meet her in Ellisville!" Aimee cried sorrowfully, as she thought how far away it was. "And it was so hard to get it all in ten words, too" (12).

Lily has always had a special relation with Aimee: "It's (Ellisville) a lovely place," said Aimee Slocum uncertainly. "You've got bumps on your face," said Lily. "Aimee, dear, you stay out of this, if you don't mind," said Mrs. Carson anxiously. "I don't know what it is comes over Lily when you come around her." Lily stared at Aimee Slocum meditatively. (9)

The terms used to describe Aimee's relation to Lily, "uncertainty", "sorrowfully", and the tears that are exchanged between them, are our only hope. It is Lily who first notices that her musician has indeed come back to get her, and she points to him from within the train "laughing softly through her fingers". Outside the train, Aimee Slocum runs into him, but she is "crying so hard" about Lily that she nearly knocks him over:

The ladies help Lily off the train, and Welty makes us feel that our sense of injustice at the prospect of taking Lily to Ellisville, as opposed to allowing her to get married, is also misplaced: "We're taking you to get married," said Mrs. Watts. "Mrs. Carson, you'd better phone up your husband right there in the station." "But I don't want to get married," said Lily, beginning to whimper. "I'm going to Ellisville" (14). Everyone has forgotten the hope chest on the train, and so Lily's hopes are left behind either way. These hopes are what is unknowable in the communication between the other characters in the story: "And whom have we the pleasure of addressing?" Mrs. Watts was shouting, while Mrs. Carson was ringing up the telephone. The band went on playing. Some of the people though Lily was on the train, and some

swore she wasn't. Everybody cheered, though, and a straw
hat was thrown into the telephone wires. (15)

WHERE IS THE VOICE COMING FROM?

The question in the title of this 1963 short story can be asked within and
without the story: whose voice is the author imitating, and furthermore,
can the voice possibly be her own? Welty conjures a slain civil rights
leaders killer from out of her own sense of his time and place, thereby
acknowledging what she might share with him. This is a triumphant act
of the imagination, and one that humanizes us, by showing that what has
necessarily happened to another always accidentally happens to us, in so
far as we share the same place. America's history is divided according to
place, and Welty's sympathy with the south is something she does not
want to, and cannot avoid: "I wrote his story (the killer's)—my fiction—
in the first person: about that character's point of view, I felt, through my
shock and revolt, I could make no mistake" (829). The translation that
occurs as she moves from "his story" to her fiction is possible because of
a shared place. She could not be wrong—she cannot help but write the
story. She appears to love all of her characters. She tells us, in her preface
to the "Collected Stories", that the voice that animates the story "comes
from within", from "living here—they were part of living here" (829).

The story begins, quite literally, from the perspective of the killer.
He is looking at a T.V, but the confusion we feel as readers, that he might
be talking about the world, is the very state of mind that makes his crime
possible:

> I says to my wife, "You can reach and turn it off. You don't
> have to set and look at a black nigger face no longer than you
> want to, or listen to what you don't want to hear. It's still a
> free country" (727).

The relation to the T.V. is an image of the man's relation to life, and
Welty places us where this fiction becomes fact. This is also the
intersection of one's private and public life. A local prejudice is expanded
because of the incursion of the national perspective into the local by the
media, just as that prejudice will achieve national notoriety and be
reported on the television, and in Welty's story. Of course, a local

prejudice can become a larger political movement, and even define a place. We are determined, and our freedom is determined, by the place that we share. The blacks, the killer might argue, are here accidentally. I am here necessarily. We are all here necessarily. We are hunted by place. The perspective we now have on the killer exposes a paradox that is integral to democracy: that hate could be an aspect of freedom, or at least another side of the enforcement of the right to tolerate. In the story, a man assassinates a black man in the town of Thermoplylae, a place name that evokes the battles of democracies and of the past.

In the story, Welty reveals a scene of revelation for the killer—he recounts the moment of watching television, and realizes the precise moment he came up with the idea for the killing. Virtually turning off a person's life inspire the idea of really doing so, and the killer's intimate knowledge of his town is an integral part of his plan: "I could find right exactly where in Thermopylae that nigger's living that's asking for equal time. And without a bit of trouble to me".... "And I ain't saying it might not be because that's pretty close to where I live" (727). The man's sense of himself is similar to his sense of his relation to the placement of his home—the same can be said for his own rehearsal of his motives. Is he doing what he is doing for the sake of a political movement, or for himself? He claims the latter: "I done what I done for my own pure-D satisfaction" (728).

The killer's self-reflection is rendered as an act of memory. The following is his account of waiting for the man he is about to kill to come home:

> As soon as I heard wheels, I knowed who was coming. That was him and bound to be him. It was the right nigger heading in a new white car up his driveway towards his garage with the light shining, but stopping before he got there, maybe not to wake 'em. That was him. I knowed it when he cut off the car lights and put his foot out and I knowed him standing dark against the light. I knowed him then like I know me now. I knowed him even by his still, listening back. (728)

The scene is strange because the killer imagines the black man in the midst of an act of caring. The man has taken great pains to quiet his approach to his house, so as not to disturb his family, and the killer cannot help but recount that fact, almost unconsciously. We feel that this imaginative act must be done unthinkingly, because of a principle of memory enunciated by the killer that is made to feel itself almost murderous: "I knowed him then like I know me now". This sure and particular knowledge is strange, especially considering that fact that the killer tells us the black man is previously unknown to him: "Never seen him before, never seen him since, never seen anything of his black face but his picture, never seen his face alive, any time at all, or anywheres, and didn't want to, need to, never hope to see that face and never will" (728). The possibility of personhood as been cut off for the black man in advance, almost as if by prophecy: "That was him and bound to be him.... He had to be the one". This is one of the finest representations of what prejudice is that we possess.

The killer understands his own desires through the image he creates of the black man. It is almost as if the only way he can prove that they are not equals is to kill the black man, an act that, in spite of and because of its negativity, reaffirms the potential equality of the victim: "It was mighty green where I skint over the yard getting back. That nigger wife of his, she wanted nice grass! I bet my wife would hate to pay her water bill" (729).

The killer believes that that his explanation of his motivation is accurate. He has killed, he says, purely for his own satisfaction. The story accounts for another explanation of his motives, that the killing was performed "for" his city. The personal motives of the man are haunted by political ones, just as his political motives are taken personally. The killer is strange, in that he insists over and over again that he does not want credit for the crime. While discussing a newspaper column with his wife, the following dialogue takes place:

> I says to my wife, "Find some way I don't get the credit." "He says do it for Thermopylae," she says. "Don't you ever skim the paper?" I says, "Thermopylae never done nothing for me. And I don't owe nothing to Thermopylae. Didn't do it for you. Hell, any more'n I'd do something or other for them Kennedys! I done it for my own pure-D satisfaction." (729)

Killing the black man, whose name is Roland Summers, has only made his presence greater on TV. The perpetrator of the crime remains anonymous. The relationship between being known and being anonymous in the story is a curious one. Either you are known, like a family member, or you are in the public. Towards the end of the story, the killer relates the following tale:

> Once, I run away from home. And there was an ad for me, come to be printed in our county weekly. My mother paid for it. It was from her. It says: "Son: You are not being hunter for anything but to find you." That time, I come on back home. (732)

In the phrase "It's still a free country", a man defines his rights as a person in terms of the history of his place. The phrase is used to justify feelings of intolerance, and is all the more meaningful for being applied to feelings of hate. The use of the word "still" implies a sense of the origins of America, a place defined by its refusal to accept a tyrannical definition of a people's duties. For the main character of this story, this political vision is felt very personally, and we must be very careful before we casually say that it is felt incorrectly, or that the vision is misapplied. The personal and private and the public and political are, according to the terms of the story, linked inexorably, and especially in feeling: "Even the President, so far, he can't walk in my house without being invited, like he's my daddy, just to say whoa. Not yet!" (732).

The killer, in order to carry out his mission, must imagine and interfere with the domestic rhythms of his victim, an imaginative act that would seem to betray his claim that black people lack humanity. There is something shared between them, the common ground of local custom. This act is at the center of the story. The killer notices a number of details about the black man's life, details which are, by comparison, absent from his own:

> And there was his light on, waiting for me. In his garage, if you please. His car's gone. He's out planning still some other ways to do what we tell 'em they can't. (727)

The black man's wife has left the light on to guide her husband home, an act that the killer's wife fails to perform:

I says, "You didn't even leave a light burning when you went to bed. So how was I supposed to even get me home or pull buddy's truck up safe in our front yard?" (729–730)

THE OPTIMIST'S DAUGHTER

In her memoir, Welty tells us that her own father was a grand optimist, and defines the term as "seeing life in terms of the future" (934). Her father literalized this description, as someone who sold life insurance for a living. He was someone who had been touched early by the loss of his mother, and so Welty identifies his sense of mortality generally with his sense of the mortality of a parent. He was primarily an optimist, however, in that he believed that the "certainty" of a child's education was of the utmost importance. Laurel, the main character in "The Optimist's Daughter", is our own glimpse into Welty's meditation on what is necessary in the inheritance a father leaves a daughter. As a provider, a father works to insure the life of his children, and in the book Judge McKelva, the father, is shown to have done so ways that were, for him, unforeseeable. Welty is interested in these unpredictable consequences of a life, because she hears in them the workings of memory. The book is a contest of memory, and it reveals the father's life as one of anticipation. The work of this anticipation is reformed as the memory of a daughter.

The judge who is the father figure in "The Optimist's Daughter" is being cared for by a Dr. Courtland, as he is having problems with his vision. When vision is in question, problems can be either real or imagined—seeing things does not necessarily mean that there is something wrong with your physical eye. Judge McKelva is having hallucinatory episodes: "Nate," Judge McKelva was saying, "the trouble may be I'm not as young as I used to be. But I'm ready to believe it's something wrong with my eyes" (4). A problem with his eyes means, pragmatically and spiritually, that he cannot see to tell time, and must trust others to tell it to him. A crucial difference between his daughter, Laurel, and his second wife, Fay, is thereby demonstrated. Laurel takes great care each morning to tell her father what time it is, and gradually registers the extent to which marking the passage of time has come to occupy his entire mind. Fay, however, selfishly believes in the impersonality of this act, and impatiently tries to speed up his recovery.

Laurel begins to feel a kind of sympathy for her father that is put forth by the dual resonance of the word watch—it sounds exactly like watch, in the sense of a timepiece: "Fay leaned over the bed and said, "I'm glad you can't see yourself, hon." Judge McKelva gave out a shocking and ragged sound, a snore, and firmed his mouth. He asked, "What's the time, Fay?" "That sounds more like you," she said, but didn't tell him the time" (16–7). Watching is a way of registering another person's time, and so is a synonym for sympathy.

In the novel, the ritualistic mourning and memory of the Judge by the women he has known and fathered seems to eclipse the man himself, and stands as a perfect image of how he was even in life. As readers, we struggle to imagination if the story would feel much different if the judge were alive. His daughter Laurel reads to him as he lays ill in the hospital, and their relationship transforms—"He opened his mouth and swallowed what she offered him with the obedience of an old man—obedience! She felt ashamed to let him act out the part in front of her" (22). Her father was always a patient man, but now seems to "lie in a dream of patience" (24), a condition liberalized by the forced rest required of him during his stay in the hospital. He loves to be read to, and the passivity he embodies is coming to represent more and more a passivity in relation to the women in his life who may always have been present: "Laurel felt reluctant to leave her father now in the afternoons. She stayed and read. Nickolas Nickelby had seemed as endless to her as time must seem to him, and it had now been arranged between them, without words, that she was to sit there beside him and read—but silently to herself" (25). The loving nature of Laurel's relation to her father is troubled by the presence of his second wife, a women who is younger than her. Laurel's burden is now to encourage her father's recovery, and after he is dead, to recover his memory: "He, who had been the declared optimist, had not once expressed hope. Now it was she who was offering it to him. And it might be false hope" (29).

Laurel's patience with her father is equaled by his new wife's impatience, and it is unclear but possible that this is what kills the judge: "She (Fay, the new wife) laid hands on him! She said if he didn't snap out of it, she'd—" (32). The shock of this episode, at the very least, contributes to the Judge's death, and it becomes time for Laurel to participate in and monitor the act of mourning: "At the sting in her eyes, she remembered for him that there must be no tears in his, and she reached to put her hand into his open hand and press it gently" (33). She monitor's the act because of the way she is situated in relation to it. She is the Judge's daughter, but she lives away from her hometown, in Chicago. Like Welty, she is born of a small town but possessed by the urge to travel. Things seem different to her—in the waiting room of the hospital after her father's death, she observes another family's ordeal: "We'll pout it down him!" cried the mother. "He ain't going to stand a chance against us!" The family laughed louder, as if there could be no helping it. Some of the other families joined in. It seemed to Laurel that in another moment the whole waiting room would dissolve itself in waiting-room laughter" (40). Terms that are ordinary for a hospital, like patient and waiting room, are refigured by Welty from the perspective of an optimist's daughter, and made to sound like time: "Dr. Courtland stood in the doorway, the weight of his watch in his hand" (40). A hospital is a certain literalization of a relation to time, it is a way of telling time. Laurel and Fay mitigate this reality differently. Laurel with care, Fay with impatience. Nobody really knows Fay's age, "Perhaps she was forty, and so younger than Laurel" (26). Fay didn't even understand why Laurel came to see her marry her father. She is married to him, but still a stranger, and not only because she has to compete with the memory of Laurel's mother.

Laurel has already suffered great loss in her life with her mother and her husband. Death is a way to register the passage of time, and Laurel's sense of time has shifted with her father's demise: "Eventually, Laurel saw that her father had accepted her uselessness with her presence all along. What occupied his full mind was time itself; time passing: he was concentrating. She was always conscious, once she knew, of the effort being made in this room, hour after hour, from his motionless bed; and she was conscious of time along with him, setting her inner chronology with his, more or less as if they needed to keep in step for a long walk ahead of them.... Laurel sat so that this light fell into her lap onto her book, and Judge McKelva, holding himself motionless, listened to her read, then turn the page, as if he were silently counting, and knew each page by its number" (20).

After her father's death, Laurel returns to her family home to find herself in the midst of an entire county's grieving process. Judge McKelva was well known, and nearly everyone is there. The remnants of Laurel's wedding are there too: "All six of Laurel's bridesmaids, as they still called themselves, were waiting on the station platform" (49). In addition to the memories of her husband, Laurel is also forced to share the house with Fay, who is now its defacto proprietor if not its just spiritual one. Judge McKelva is remembered only through the remembered discrepancy between his first and second wives. On her first night home after her father's death, Laurel's friends and relatives have gathered, leaving their husbands at home so as not to double her sense of loss, and remind her as she grieves for a father that she is already missing a husband. The women perform a kind of duty of grief that is best described by Laurel's response upon entering her pantry: "Well, I didn't know I was giving a reception" (53). Present allegiances are being defined in the wake of the Judge's death—Laurel's people tell Fay very clearly that they are there now for "Laurel's mother's sake" (53). Society itself seems to be held together by a woman's ability to believe in the death of her husband. When one women expresses disbelief, and grief at her own loss, another takes responsibility: "All right, I'll believe it for you" (55).

Laurel's first night without her parent's in her childhood house contains an echo of Welty's own childhood:

> When Laurel was a child, in this room and in this bed where she lay now, she closed her eyes like this and the rhythmic, nighttime sound of the two beloved reading voices came rising in turn up the stairs every night to reach her. She could hardly fall asleep, she tried to keep awake, for pleasure. She cared about her own books, but she cared more for their, which meant their voices. In the lateness of the night, their two voices reading to each other where she could hear them, never letting a silence divide or interrupt them, combined into one unceasing voice and wrapped her around as she listened, as still as if she were still asleep.

Lest we forget, Fay too is sleeping in the house, in the same place if not in the same time as Laurel:

> Fay slept farther away tonight than in the Hibiscus (Hotel where they stayed when Judge McKelva was in the hospital)—they could not hear each other in this house—But

nearer in a different way. She was sleeping in the bed where
Laurel was born; And where her mother had died. What
Laurel listened for tonight was the striking of the mantel
clock downstairs in the parlor. It never came. (58)

What Laurel was listening for was the memory of a familiar time. If she
had heard it, a sympathetic echo would have sounded louder to her than
a strange absence of time. Time, however, is still registered by the
absence of familiar sounds, as the pulse of Laurel's memory supplies a
place for the sound of a clock that someone has forgotten to wind. What
is different about Laurel and Fay has to do with listening, and with sound.
Laurel listens to her father's condition as patient, and hears his situation.
Fay listens only to herself, and so cannot speak to or hear another: "What
Fay told Laurel now, nearly every afternoon at the changeover, was
almost the same thing. Her flattery and her disparagement sounded just
alike" (27). Laurel reads to her father when he is asleep, Fay will not tell
him what time it is when he is awake. When Judge McKelva does die, she
only registers the death on her own terms: "All on my birthday. Nobody
told me this was what was going to happen to me!" (44).

The next morning is the wake, with casket open to display her
father's body. Laurel wanted to "protect her father" from the people's
eyes, but Fay wants the casket open. Somehow, seeing the Judge's dead
body, perfunctorily, is only knowing it, and not really recognizing it.
We are reminded that the Judge has spared his first wife this indignity.
Throughout the story, we are forbidden access to the Judge's first wife,
or only told about her in statements cast in an impossible comparison.
She is, and this is repeated throughout the novel, "different", and the
similarity of her demise to that of her husband's is more than a
coincidence. At an occasion like this, people are inclined to tell stories
about the deceased. They are attempting to tell the ending of a man's
life, and so inaugurate the celebration of him in memory. Laurel
remains committed to a version of her father, in memory, that she feels
is correct. To say and believe as much about her vision seems to enlarge
her and her father both. Laurel feels that lies are now being propagated
about her father, and that her testimony is needed, "as though he were
in process of being put on trial in here instead of being viewed in his
casket" (83). Laurel sense of what is true and false in the memory of her
father is equal to whatever is meaningful in ritual. Women are the

victims and the guardians of ritual in the novel: "A good thing you reminded me! Said Mrs. Bolt. "My husband hasn't yet rehearsed his Sunday sermon to me, and he's got just today and tomorrow" (108). Laurel's father, as a judge, tried to rehearse the theatre out of the courtroom. His funeral was just another spectacle: "She wanted nothing but the best for her husband's funeral, only the most expensive casket, the most choice cemetery plot—" "Choice! It looked right out on the Interstate! Those horrible trucks made so much whine, not a thing Dr. Bolt was saying could be heard. Even from our good seats," said Miss Tennyson (110).

The hope of a father is the memory of a daughter, and the memory of Laurel's wedding haunts the funeral of her father. The bridesmaids who were a part of her wedding ceremony are responsible for her visit home, and insist "We're grieving with you!" (127). Laurel's trip home has become a visit, rather than a return: "She smiled her thanks and kissed them all. She would see the bridesmaids once more. At noon tomorrow they were coming for her, all six, to drive her to her plane" (127). The memory of Laurel's marriage is always present during her visit home, and almost invades the work she needs to do for her father. The representatives of a past ritual, bridesmaids, are the guardians of Laurel's visit, even as they seem to haunt it. The relation between the two rituals, Laurel's marriage and her father's funeral, is as the difference between what is past and what is memory:

> And it occurred to Laurel that Fay might already have been faithless to her Father's memory. "I know you aren't anything to the past," she said. "You can't do anything to it now." And neither am I; and neither can I, she though, although it has been everything and done everything to me, everything for me. The past is not more open to help or hurt than was Father in his coffin. The past is like him, impervious, and can never be awakened. It is memory that is the somnambulist. It will come back in its wounds from across the world, like Phil, calling us by our names and demanding its rightful tears. It will never be impervious. The memory can be hurt, time and again—but in that may lie its final mercy. As long as it's vulnerable To the living moment, it lives for us, and while it lives, and while we are able, we can give it up its due. (179)

Eudora Welty's fiction is organized according to principle she called "confluence", which means the writer's responsibility to testify to the possible patterns in life. She found refuge and strength for her writing in the memory of her own family life, and a vision of time and place that, while a tribute to her respect for her origins, grants the imagination the greatest possible inward freedom. Discovery is always haunted by memory for Welty, just as memory is the only possible beginning of discovery. It is this relation which gives value to what is personal while enriching what is shared.

WORK CITED

Kreyling, Michael and Richard Ford. *Library of America 102: Eudora Welty Stories, Essays, and A Memoir*. Library of America Publishing, September, 1998.

WILLIAM M. JONES

Name and Symbol in the
Prose of Eudora Welty

Although most critics tend to classify Eudora Welty as only a good regional writer, a careful look at her yet unexplained symbols will, perhaps, make it clear that she has something more in mind than regional atmosphere. The tortuous path she sets for her reader leads through a forest of symbol, but there is a path and there is a reward at its end. From her earliest published work to her latest collection of stories Miss Welty has drawn heavily upon the worlds of myth and folklore[1] and, while handling many of the same motifs again and again, has consistently absorbed them more and more fully into her own meaning, so that in her most successful work it is impossible to say that here is Cassiopeia and here Andromeda. The reader can only be aware that these legendary figures, along with similar ones from Germanic, Celtic, Sanskrit, and numerous other folk sources, are suggested by the characters that Miss Welty is drawing.

Miss Welty, although never alluding directly to her own method of writing, has occasionally made statements that would seem to justify her use of folk material as source: "And of course the great stories of the world are the ones that seem new to their readers on and on, always new because they keep their power of revealing something."[2] According to this quotation, she might feel justified in presenting a story firmly based in antiquity in terms familiar to her own generation. Thus, her

From *Southern Folklore Quarterly* 22 (December 1958): 173–185. © 1958 by *Southern Folklore Quarterly*. Reprinted by permission.

seemingly new stories might draw upon the great stories of all time for their "power of revealing something."

The something revealed in these old stories would seem to be, according to Miss Welty's selection from them, true characters, whose validity has been proved in folk stories of many cultures and many ages. Quite consciously Miss Welty has taken the characters common to several mythological systems and translated them into present-day Mississippians. Although a faintly fantastic element remains in her stories, her characters and her atmosphere are too thoroughly Southern to be mistaken for those of Siegfried's Germany or Perseus's Greece. So typically Southern are they, in fact, that many critics damn her for her provincial approach to life.[3]

By patterning her characters closely after folk heroes Miss Welty has avoided exactly such a strictly regional approach as that for which she has been blamed. Since her first published story she has been working toward a fusion of the universal mythic elements embodied in various culture-heroes with the regional world that she knows first-hand. The effect of this attempt on her work and her degree of success with it may be followed throughout her work.

The most obvious advantage to such an approach to fiction may be seen in the stories of her first collection, *A Curtain of Green* (1941). The last story in this Collection, "A Worn Path," may appear at first to be a sweet story of an old Negro woman who makes periodic trips into Natchez for medicine for her grandson. But sweet stories are readily available in women's magazines everywhere. Miss Welty has added depth to this one by building, closely upon a legend that was told first about an embodiment of the Egyptian sun-god and retold later by medieval Christians to glorify the resurrection of Christ. The Old Negro woman, Phoenix Jackson, like the original Phoenix, is definitely golden: "Her skin had ... a golden color ..., and the two knobs of her cheeks were illuminated by a yellow burning under the dark ... her hair ... with an odor of copper."[4] Just as the Egyptian Phoenix is guided back to its home every five hundred years to renew itself by being consumed in fire, so the modern Phoenix sees, at the end of her journey, a gold seal in a gold frame, "which matched the dream that was hung up in her head." Then "there came a flicker and then a flame," after which "Phoenix rose carefully." With this Mississippi Phoenix it is love that renews and love that will lead the ancient and eternally young one back down the worn path.

In other stories in this collection Miss Welty also makes use of a specific name from folk knowledge as a point of departure for the story itself.[5] In such a story as "Clytie" Miss Welty presents a Southern spinster with a very appropriate name, but it also happens to be the name of a jealous girl in Ovid's *Metamorphoses* who, having pined away because of her unrequited love for the sun-god, eventually became a sunflower. Miss Welty's very description of Clytie gives a suggestion of just such a huge sunflower: "On her head was one of the straw hats from the furnishing store, with an old black satin ribbon pinned to it to make it a better hat, and tied under the chin. Now under the force of the rain, while the ladies watched, the hat slowly began to sag down on each side until it looked even more absurd and done for." Not only does Miss Welty know her Ovid; she also knows sunflowers in the rain.

The rest of the story even more explicitly carries out the myth idea: "With this small, peaceful face still in her mind, rosy like these flames, like an inspiration which drives all other thoughts away, Clytie had forgotten herself and had been obliged to stand where she was in the middle of the road." Just so, Ovid's Clytie "never stirred from the ground; all she did was to gaze on the face of the sungod...." To support the idea of the dependence on Greek myth even more, Miss Welty introduces another name, Lethe. It is old Lethy, a Negro woman, who finds Clytie drowned in the rain barrel. What promise for Clytie's soul that she is discovered by the river of forgetfulness! And yet also, what an appropriate name for a Southern Negro!

In these first stories the myth from which Miss Welty has drawn her material is easily recognized. Once the first hint in the story is found, the source material can easily be observed throughout the rest of the story, hidden certainly under Southern trappings but observably present, nevertheless. At first Miss Welty seems to have thought of a myth, then thought of ways in which to modernize and southernize it. The stories constructed in this manner are not as transparently derivative as might be expected, since Miss Welty from the beginning of her career has been a marvelously skilled and careful craftsman. Even in stories where only one myth is used the Southern veneer is so thick that the basic material is hardy recognizable. Yet, satisfactorily enough, its unrecognized presence still gives a weight to the story that it might not otherwise have had. Miss Welty, at least, was aware of the myth used, and even if the reader misses its presence, its availability may well be felt.

In her next work, *The Robber Bridegroom* (1942), Miss Welty reveals her folk sources more clearly and at the same time goes a step further toward combining various myths and legends in order to avoid the one to one equating which she had practiced in *A Curtain of Green*. The title and basic plot, as well as the main characters, are almost direct borrowings from "Der Rauberbräutigam," one of the stories in Grimm's collection.[6] In both stories the bridegroom lives far out in the dark forest. In Grimm a raven warns "Kehr um, kehr um, du junge Braut, / du bist in einem Mörderhaus." Miss Welty changes this warning only slightly: "Turn again, my bonny, / Turn away home." Miss Welty's robbers, like those in Grimm, kill a young girl. In Grimm she is cut to pieces. In *The Robber Bridegroom* she is an Indian girl who is first raped.

But perhaps the most significant similarity in the two stories is the cutting off of a finger. In both stories the dead girl's finger is cut off, in Grimm because that was the easiest way of obtaining the ring on it. In Miss Welty's story, however, "none of them saw where the finger went or hunted for it, for it had no ring on it." This direct echo of the Grimm story suggests that here Miss Welty fully expects that her readers be aware of her sources. Otherwise, much of the significance of the retelling of the story is lost. Any careful reader should have curiosity enough to wonder why an author would give such a negative piece of information as the absence of a ring from a finger.

Many more parallels between the two stories could be pointed out, but they are easily observable once the basic similarity has been established. To this story Miss Welty has added many other legendary features: the wicked step-mother, a box with a talking head inside, a Salome who dances, casting off one "petticoat" after another. And to these general folklore characters she adds an important one from Mississippi folklore, an old acquaintance of Davy Crockett himself, Mike Fink, the last of the keelboatmen.[7] Fink serves an essential function in the novel. At the beginning of the story he introduces the heroine's father to the robber bridegroom, and at the end he serves to reunite the two lovers. To this fantastic[8] conglomeration of legends Miss Welty adds her own serious comments on the struggle of good and evil within the individual human spirit and, possibly most important of all, the power of love to remake a personality and overcome all obstacles.

In *The Robber Bridegroom* Miss Welty is clearly reaching for a more complex use of folk material than that of *A Curtain of Green*. This complicating, fusing process continued in her next group of stories, *The Wide Net* (1943). As she absorbs more and more folk elements into her work it becomes increasingly difficult to recognize any one specific source. The stories themselves take on more of the general characteristics of the folk tale and thus become less obviously stories that draw on folk material.

The introduction of almost inhuman cruelty into such a story as "At the Landing" recalls stories from Grimm in which girls are cut into pieces and salted. This story concludes with the mass rape of the leading character, Jenny, by fishermen who go in to her where she is imprisoned in a chicken house, while outside the younger boys "took their turns throwing knives with a dull *pit* at the tree." Such cruelty as this would be almost unbearable except for another folk-tale characteristic, the remoteness of the characters. In spite of numerous realistic details they remain in this collection rather aloof, neither purely symbolic nor purely human, only distant from the present-day world. They seem more like Rapunzel than like Liza of Lambeth.

Part of their remoteness may be attributed to still other folk-tale characteristics. In the title story, "The Wide Net," the sudden action and lack of thoughtful motivation show close kinship to folk tales. While walking in the woods, the hero, without reason, "ran at a rabbit and caught it in his hands." A king of snakes suddenly rises from the Pearl River; a man begins dancing with a catfish at his belt; another man drinks water from his mother-in-law's well. All these seemingly unmotivated actions are direct echoes from mythology[9] and, according to Erich Fromm,[10] become meaningful if viewed on a symbolic level.

Miss Welty seems still to have been experimenting with the stories in "The Wide Net," for along side these stories that add something of the form of folk tales to the material derived from them, there are others that, while also based on legend, are more obviously Southern like her first ones. In "Asphodel" the name of the immortal plant is the only really legendary feature of the story. The discovery by three old maids on a picnic of the lusty Do McInnis, "naked as an old goat," and their escape from "billy-goats, and nanny-goats, old goats and young, a whole thriving herd," is all good Southern humor. But, with the aid of vague classical hints and all those goats, the reader gets the impression that one of the three old maids may someday dance with the satyrs or worship at Bacchus' shrine: "But Phoebe laughed aloud as they made the curve.

Her voice was soft, and she seemed to be still in a tender dream and an unconscious celebration—as though the picnic were not already set rudely in the past, but were the enduring and intoxicating present, still the phenomenon, the golden day.

In her next work, *Delta Wedding* (1946), Miss Welty seems to have doubts no longer about what to do with her sources. She has almost completely obscured them under a wealth of Southern atmosphere. As in her earlier work there are key names,[11] but the majority of them have nothing to do with the plot and do not come directly from folklore. The key names are there, however, and as usual they point the way to an understanding of Miss Welty's form and purpose.

On the surface the story is only one of a Southern family, concerned because their daughter is about to marry a common overseer. A more careful examination reveals two devices that Miss Wetly has used before. These devices give meaning to what otherwise might have been only a somewhat rambling, atmospheric, overly detailed story of Southern plantation life in the 1920's.

First, the reader notices that Mr. Rondo, who appeared in "Why I Live at the P.O.,"[12] is now a minister who is to marry the daughter and the overseer. It is to him that the story of Uncle George's saving the feeble-minded child Maureen from the train is first told. The story, thus set up, returns again and again in its rondo-like movement to the original statement: George stands on a trestle holding Maureen, who has caught her foot. The oncoming train, the Yellow Dog, stops in time to avoid an accident, but George's wife resents George's action. She cries, "George Fairchild, you didn't do this for *me!*"

Once Mr. Rondo has heard this tale, he disappears until the wedding. Before the final treatment of the train theme, however, Mr. Rondo appears again. This time he rides with the Fairchilds and Laura McRaven when the Yellow Dog stops again to let them by. He is then put out at the church stile, where he is last seen taking out his watch, "which ... seemed to have stopped." Then, with a sudden shift, the next scene begins, "'Poor Ellen,' said Tempe, clasping her softly, her delicate fragrant face large and serious...." And Aunt Tempe (tempi) takes over to bring the times of the Fairchilds to a close.

There is little doubt that Aunt Tempe sets the time in the novel just as Mr. Rondo sets the form. On Aunt Tempe's first appearance Miss Welty emphasized the idea of time: "Aunt Tempe, in a batik dress and a

vibratingly large hat, entered (keeping time) and kissed all the jumping children." And in the background of Aunt Tempe's conversation the reader is always aware of music from a distant piano. She it is who regrets the children's not taking piano lessons; she it is who sometimes speeds up the action, sometimes slows it down. But her function is never obvious, nor is Mr. Rondo's. They are first of all real characters in a real world.

The second device which Miss Welty has used before is the piling up of names from the same source. Any one of these names in itself might not have special meaning, but their combined weight leads to an interesting source discovery. The names Battle, Lady Clare, Ellen, Inverness, Marmion, plus three excerpts from Scottish songs on one page, leave no doubt that Miss Welty was thinking of Scott's *Marmion* when she wrote *Delta Wedding*.

Any attempt, however, to compare the plot or theme of the two works fails. Miss Welty's Marmion is a house which rightfully belongs to Laura, but which is given instead to Dabney, the girl about to marry the overseer. Scott's Marmion is a villainous knight who forsakes Lady Clare, wife of a man he has supposedly killed, and who finally dies in battle at Flodden Field. It is definitely not the plot here that Miss Welty uses. But the names, the songs, and the fact that Scott's poem ends on September 9 and Miss Welty begins *Delta Wedding* on September 10 may suggest that she is taking up where Scott left off. Scott's introductory "Advertisement" says something very similar to what Miss Welty might have said, but did not: "Any historical narrative, far more an attempt at epic composition, exceeded his [the author's] plan of a romantic tale; yet he may be permitted to hope, from the popularity of 'The Lay of the Last Minstrel,' that an attempt to paint the manners of the feudal times, upon a broader scale, and in the course of a more interesting story, will not be unacceptable to the public."

In other words, Miss Welty's second long work, like Scott's second long narrative poem, deals more with description than with the narrative elements which dominated their first works, is more simply a romantic tale to please the public. This interpretation might be developed with the idea also that Miss Welty is analyzing "manners of feudal times" as they exist in the South. And the two who rise above these regional and outmoded manners, Uncle George and Laura, both have a universality that causes the Yellow Dog, a local train, to stop out of respect for them.

It almost seems that Miss Welty's mind dwelt on *Marmion* even after the completion of *Delta Wedding*. Although she might easily have got her information from any other source of Arthurian legend, the earlier argument for Marmion suggests that when she decided to name the town Morgana in her next group of short stories, *The Golden Apples* (1949), she was thinking of the introduction to the first canto of *Marmion*:

> But thou, my friend, cans't fitly tell,
> (For few have read romance so well,)
> How still the legendary lay
> O'er poet's bosom holds its sway;
> How on the ancient minstrel strain
> Time lays his palsied hand in vain;
> And how our hearts at doughy deeds,
> By warriors wrought in steely weeds,
> Still throb for fear and pity's sake;
> As when the Champion of the Lake
> Entered Morgana's fated house....

This quotation, which ends with the name that became Miss Welty's imaginary Mississippi town in *The Golden Apples*, expresses her own idea of literature. She herself has supported the idea that the good stories, the true stories, are not dulled by time. Nowhere does she better illustrate the truth of this idea than in *The Golden Apples*. Here, for the first time in the short story, she succeeds in fusing a number of legends so completely that her Southerners take on the basic attributes of these legendary characters, engage in the same general sort of activity.

The entire series of stories seems to deal in a general way with the Perseus legend.[13] In the first story, "Shower of Gold, "Jove's visit to Danaë in the form of a shower of gold is suggested in Mrs. Fate Rainey's description of her first view of Snowdie MacLain after Snowdie had met King MacLain in Morgan's Woods, probably the woods of King Arthur's half-sister Morgan la Feé: "Me and Lady May both had to just stop and look at her. She looked like more than only the news of her pregnancy had come over her. It was like a shower of something had struck her, like she'd been caught out in something bright. It was more than the day.... I remember it was Easter time and how the pasture was all spotty there behind her little blue skirt in sweet clover. He [King] sold tea and spices, that's what it was."

Already in this quotation it is evident that Miss Welty is fusing elements common to various mythological systems. The Easter reference, the blue skirt, the clover, and the spices add to the pagan myth the idea of the Virgin Mary's own discovery that she was to give birth to a hero. The narrator of the story is all Southern, except her rather significant name; but the tale she tells echoes through ages and ages of myth, Greek, Hebrew, Egyptian, British, Germanic, and Egyptian. What Miss Welty seems to have striven consciously for in her first stories, the fusion of many myths with Southern life, takes place here so frequently and effortlessly as to seem almost unavoidable.

In the second story, "June Recital," the legends become so intermingled that it is impossible to tell if her character Cassie is Cassiopeia, Cassandra, or a combination of numerous other mythical figures. Miss Welty finally seems to have succeeded in finding a successful balance between her Southern atmosphere and the numerous characters from folk knowledge, now thoroughly merged.

In this story, too, Miss Welty creates one of her most effective symbols, built, like the characters, on ages of myth. Miss Eckhart, who is trying to burn down King MacLain's old house where she used to live, "worshiped her metronome." Old Man Moody and Fatty Bowles want to destroy "the obelisk with its little moving part and its door open." "Old Man Moody stumped over and picked it up and held it upon the diagonal, posing, like a fisherman holding a funny-looking fish to have come out of Moon Lake." To those acquainted with folklore, Miss Welty's use of the Egyptian obelisk and the Hindu fish to support her own new phallic symbol is an amazing accomplishment. And, when the two frightened men throw away this symbol, the young man, Loch, retrieves it:

> On his hands he circled the tree and the obelisk waited in the weeds, upright. He stood up and looked at it.
> Its ticker was outside it.
> He felt charmed like a bird, for the ticking stick went like a tail, a tongue, a wand ....
> When he examined it, he saw the beating stick to be a pendulum that instead of hanging down stuck upwards....

He held still for a while, while nothing was ticking. Nothing but the crickets. Nothing but the train going through, ticking its, two cars over the Big Black Bridge.

This creation of symbol and expansion to the ticking pounding movement of the rest of life is a good example of how Miss Welty can pour new meaning into old mythic material. And yet Robert Daniel, writing in the *Hopkins Review*, can simply say that the metronome is "a symbol of time" and leave it at that.[14]

Not only does Miss Welty use myth to best advantage for the creation of symbol and character in *The Golden Apples*, she also expresses most clearly here an idea common to folklore which holds a central position in much of her work, the idea that a descent into the depths results in a fuller awareness of life. These descents are numerous both in the work of Miss Welty and in folklore. Loch Morrison, the retriever of the metronome in "June Recital," dives into the depths of Moon Lake in the story "Moon Lake" in order to save one of the girls, Easter; Laura, one of the leading characters in *Delta Wedding*, falls into the Yazoo River; William Wallace in "The Wide Net" dives far below the surface of the Pearl River; and Virgie Rainey; the Virgin figure, who is to feel the fertilizing power of the rain at the end of *The Golden Apples*, had also swum beneath the surface of the river: "Virgie had reached the point where in the next moment she might turn into something without feeling it shock her. She hung suspended in the Big Black River as she would know to hang suspended in felicity."

In each instance some new revelation about life is the result of the descent into depths, just as in folklore the person who eats of the charmed fish or who goes beneath the surface of the water comes up with knowledge that leads him to riches or success.

Although it is in *The Golden Apples* that the descent is most emphasized, it was also treated thoroughly in "The Wide Net," where, partly because of the less thorough fusion of the folk elements, they appear most clearly. William Wallace's River is the Pearl River. Serpents are supposed to hold pearls under their tongues and, on warm days, spit them into the river for a larger serpent to catch. William Wallace holds the eel that is, of course, a fairly common phallic symbol, and for a moment he holds the green plant which he brought up from the river bottom. In myth this plant would have held the semen of the god. Miss

Welty even introduces the King of the Snakes into the story. At the end of the story sexual adjustment between William Wallace and his pregnant wife is the riches gained. But at the close of the story she smiles at him, "as if she were smiling down on him." Miss Welty may be suggesting that William Wallace's descent into the depths will make his wife the mother of a hero, a not uncommon occurrence in folk stories.[15]

According to Miss Welty, the riches gained form the descent are frequently a fuller understanding of nature. This coming into harmony with nature is often manifested, as with William Wallace, in a more satisfactory sexual adjustment. Just as William Wallace and Loch Morrison gain from their descent, those who do not descend are denied riches. Nina Carmichael and Jenny Love, watching Loch undress after his life-saving expedition into the depths of Moon Lake, feel that they will always be old maids. And after Laura returns from her descent into the Yazoo River she sees the unhappy Dabney, who is wearing "a beautiful floating dress." Dabney will never be able to dive beneath the surface in a floating dress.

In *The Golden Apples*, then, there is this division of the characters into those who can descend and those who cannot, and there is also the reliance in all the stories on the basic idea of the Perseus legend. The other stories in the collection, significant to the legend as they are, can be passed over lightly here since, if they are compared with the Perseus myth and the Grimm story "The Two Brothers," their general significance comes through. "The Whole World Knows" deals with the unsuccessful brother told of in the Grimm story and "Music from Spain" deals with the successful one. In "Music from Spain" the names are significant for both the Perseus story (Aeolian Hall) and the Grimm tale (Bertsinger's Jewelers and fish eggs). These names are added references to butterflies more frequent than any yet seen in Miss Welty's work,[16] a symbolic method based on folklore that emphasizes Eugene's success in the story.

In the final story, "The Wanderers," Miss Welty offers her clearest indication of what she has attempted in *The Golden Apples* and suggests, indirectly, what she has been striving for in everything else that she has written: "It [Miss Eckhart's picture] showed Perseus with the head of the Medusa. 'The same thing as Siegfried and the Dragon,' Miss Eckhart had occasionally said, as if explaining second-best. Around the picture— which sometimes blindly reflected the window by its darkness—was a frame enameled with flowers, which was always self-evident—Miss Eckhart's pride. In that moment Virgie had shorn it of its frame." Clearly, the recurrent Perseus legend, that which is eternally true about mankind, is here shorn of the flowery decorations, seen without the blinding reflection of the present. And Virgie at this moment knows the ageless.

In the last two pages of "The Wanderers" Miss Welty explains how myth may be viewed. It may be observed abstractly ("far out and endless, a constellation which the heart could read over many a night"), personally ("Miss Eckhart, whom Virgie had not, after all, hated ... had hung the picture on the wall for herself"), or socially ("The rain of fall, maybe on the whole South, for all she knew on the everywhere."). And seeing the myth in these three ways, as Miss Welty herself has seen it, "was the damnation—no, only the secret, unhurting because not caring in itself...."

With this clear expression of her attitude toward myth Miss Welty concludes the series of stories in which she achieves the most successful fusion of mythic characters and Southern setting.[17] She has, with her explanation of the Perseus picture, suggested that she is attempting in her stories to give new meaning to the oldest stories of all, not in the manner of Tennyson or O'Neill, who were satisfied with primarily one group of myths, but in her own unique manner of taking for her province the whole world of folk knowledge and compressing it into the modern South.

In all her work Miss Welty is assuming that these stories from ancient sources and the symbols involved in them contain the truth about the inmost nature of man. If she wants to reveal man as he really is and ever shall be, there is no better way then by resorting to these myths. And, in addition, by so doing she comes into contact with the world not visible, the world of imagination and beauty, the world of myth.

This mythic world, which contains an endless Medusa and an endless Perseus, says a great deal. Men may be capable of cruel deeds, but there are heroes among its men who can dive down into the depths of life, take hold of the eel, strap a catfish to their belts and dance. There are yet those men who, in spite of cruelty around them, have seen butterflies in flight, listened to the echo of the world, or felt the fall of the impregnating rain. And always there will be a Virgie, like the one at the conclusion of "The Wanderers," who will feel the power of the god in the rain and know that she will in her turn be the mother of a hero. Virgie and the old Negro woman can sit together under a Southern tree and hear as great people of all times have heard "through falling rain and the running of the horse and bear, the stroke of the leopard, the dragon's crusty slither, and the glimmer and the trumpet of the swan."

NOTES

1. Although I agree with the distinction between myth, legend and fairytale made by Susanne K. Langer, *Philosophy in a New Key* (New York, 1955), p. 144, such careful differentiation is not necessary for the purpose of this paper.

2. "The Reading and Writing of Short Stories," *Atlantic Monthly*, CLXXXIII (February, 1949), p. 54.

3. Granville Hicks quotes several such critics in "Eudora Welty," *English Journal*, XLI (November, 1952).

4. All quotations from Miss Welty are from the first editions of the novels and of the collections of stories.

5. Uranus appears in a story about a titanic Negro pianist, "Powerhouse"; the shadow of Hercules, the famous archer of antiquity, hovers over R.J. Bowman in "Death of a Traveling Salesman."

6. In his previously cited article in the *English Journal*, p. 465, Granville Hicks says that the plot is "as implausible as anything in Grimm." Apparently he did not check his Grimm to discover that the same thing was really there.

7. For a thorough treatment of Fink see Walter Blair and Franklin J. Meine, *Half Horse Half Alligator* (Chicago, 1956).

8. Miss Eunice Glenn, "Fantasy in the Fiction of Eudora Welty," *A Southern Vanguard* (New York, 1947), seems completely unaware of any of Miss Welty's "fantastic" sources.

9. Cf. subject index to Angelo de Guernatis, *Zoological Mythology* (London, 1872), 2 vols.

10. *The Forgotten Language* (New York, 1951), p. 195.

11. An old Negro woman who wanders through the story with a sack over her shoulder has the name Partheny, a suggestion of the virgin goddess Minerva and the Parthenon.

12. In "Why I Live at the P.O." (*A Curtain of Green*) two of the central characters are Uncle Rondo and Stella-Rondo. These names suggest musically the form in which a central theme is stated again and again with subordinate material interwoven between statements. The *Oxford Companion to Music* describes the form A-B-A-C-A-D-A. This circular motion of a static situation

accounts for part of the humor in she story. Stella-Rondo's return home on July 4, sets up the situation. Stella-Rondo has stolen the narrator's suitor. Now she returns to steal the narrator's place in the affections of one member of the family after another. The story moves rhythmically along in this manner. There is a summary of this rondo movement before the last figure: "So that made Mama, Papa-Daddy and the baby all on Stella-Rondo's side. Next Uncle Rondo."

13. For the most thorough treatment of all variations of the Perseus Legend see E. Sidney Hartland, *The Legend of Perseus* (London, 1894), 3 vols.

14. "The World of Eudora Welty," *The Hopkins Review*, VI (Winter, 1963), p. 56.

15. All the folk elements mentioned in this paragraph and those directly preceding are treated in detail in the previously cited *Zoological Mythology*.

16. There are a woman with a butterfly birthmarks, a Mariposa lily, and a waitress with mascaraed eyelids "like flopping black butterflies." And finally a Mr. Herring waits with Eugene's wife when he, the successful brother, returns home. Again Miss welty has put strong emphasis on the phallic symbols of folklore: butterflies and fish.

17. In Miss Welty's two latest works there are also echoes from ancient sources. Uncle Daniel Ponder of *The Ponder Heart* recalls the Biblical Daniel, who had a habit of pondering things in his heart, which beat, like Uncle Daniel's, under the finest linen garments. And Florabel, the Negro girl of the first version of "The Burning," becomes Delilah when the story appears in the collection *The Bride of the Innisfallen*. A pretty flower thus becomes a woman of another culture whose marriage into the race of the faithful (she had a white man's child) caused much turmoil for all concerned—just as Samson's Delilah did. And Florabel-Delilah finishes the story by wading into the river because "At that time it was only Friday [Venus' day] so it hadn't rained." Even without the fertilizing power of the rain she will become the mother of a hero.

HARRIET POLLACK

On Welty's Use of Allusion: Expectations and Their Revision in "The Wide Net," *The Robber Bridegroom* and *"At The Landing"*

When Eudora Welty argues that Isak Dinesen's tales all had their "start in other tales—for a tale must have its 'start,' as a good bread must" and that those starts were. most frequently from "fables ... fairy tales, stories from the Bible and the Arabian Nights and Ancient Greece and Rome" (*Eye of the Story* 262), she applies a principle she had undoubtedly learned in her bedroom studio, at work. For Welty's own habit of telling "twice-told tales" is distinctive; Welty's fictions are built on allusions to well-known stories and story patterns—and on literary, more than autobiographical, memory. She has freely appropriated legend, history, fairy tale, folklore, myth, ballad and poetry. She also has reworked southern gothic, romantic and pastoral formulas. Critics sometimes think of her as a genial southern storyteller who knows numberless time-honored tales as well as how to combine them in curious amalgamation. Scholarly readers with the classics on their minds have sometimes paid more attention to Welty's sources than to her uses of them.[1] Source hunting in itself, however, is not an adequate critical response to Welty's allusions. What needs to be attended instead is the relationship of her sources to her new text: that is, the work performed when two or more narratives are simultaneously brought to a reader's mind. Could we not, then, see her as technical innovator, experimenting with readers'

From *Southern Quarterly* 29, vol. 1 (Fall 1990): 5–31. © 1990 by the Southern Quarterly. Reprinted by permission.

expectations through her use of allusion and, simultaneously, her mixing of genres?

The first step is to map out the process characteristically initiated by Welty's allusions and then examine the specific uses she makes of that proms in three allusive fictions: "The Wide Net," *The Robber Bridegroom* and its story double, "At The Landing." Welty's fiction often evokes three types of allusion: (1) allusion that recollects a secondary literary genre and so mixes the genre of Welty's story—suggesting to a reader conflicting expectations (conflicting reading strategies) that interact; (2) allusion in its conventional sense—allusion to specific literary referents—which in Welty's case is often complicated as she calls up not one, but several, literary memories, again guiding her reader to shape conflicting expectations and to bring these into interaction; (3) interallusiveness among Welty's own fictions as another type of literary memory which her fiction evokes.

Welty's allusions, like all authors' allusions, bring together at least two texts or story patterns in readers' minds. Knowledge of the text-at-hand is modified by knowledge of a text evoked. This process has been analyzed as four discrete actions by Ziva Ben Porat: (1) recognizing the marker as closely related to—or from—a reference text; (2) identifying the evoked text, if it was not immediately recognized; (3) modifying the initial meaning of the marker to suit the next text; and (4) calling up the evoked text as a whole to form intertextual patterning. I would add a fifth process to Porat's series: (5a) calling up the entire genre to which the referent text belongs—the familiar class and pattern and all the recalled stories that belong to it—and (5b) situations in which a pattern, but no specific text, is recalled.

This revision of Forays taxonomy suggests how allusions can do much more than alter the initial reading of a single element in the fiction-at-hand. They may alter the reader's experience and understanding of the text as a whole. Welty's reader, however, often is asked to do more, to work with the associations produced by several allusions, not just one.

When readers confront an allusion, they face something like a puzzle to be solved. They must decipher not only the reference itself, but also its relevance. Those readers are likely to ask certain predictable questions. They may want to know if the fictions involved run parallel, and if the referent texts act as either plot, genre, character or motif "pointers." They may wonder which of the adapted textual patterns will be reenacted, which will be reproduced with an ironic difference and which will be totally negated. They may look to see how the earlier text will complicate the meaning of the later one and if the later text will criticize or correct the earlier one. They may be attentive to submerged aspects of the text-at-hand which now take on new emphasis as a result of intertextual patterning, an interaction that brings the reader to realize effects hovering unarticulated in the juxtaposition of two articulated presences.

Characteristically, Welty disappoints predictions built on knowledge of referent texts. She relies on obstruction as a strategy for eliciting a desired response. When her allusions arouse expectations from which her tales diverge, meaning is located in the tension between the reader's literary memory and Welty's new text. That is, allusion emphasizes difference as well as similarity. Meaning is formulated in part by reference to and obstruction of expectations based on memory. These interactions sometimes silently comment on the source fictions and, in a sense, deconstruct them.

The process by which Welty leads the reader from allusion to a strategy for unraveling meaning can be seen clearly in "The Wide Net," a short work controlled by an allusive evocation of a genre other than the realistic short story, that is by mixing of genres. Genre is conventional; it is, as E.D. Hirsch put it, "a propriety which is, on the whole, socially considerate" of the author to observe (93). The reader who unexpectedly encounters a fiction extending generic conventions may feel as disoriented as a dinner guest whose host (passes the evening without mentioning dinner. The visitor will not only be hungry but, like these readers, expectant and bewildered, too. To alter Hirsch slightly, readers also use their generic expectations as initial, prefabricated interpretive strategies. They may respond with irritation when genre expectations are frustrated, exactly as if they had been denied an expected courtesy. Welty's allusive evocation of more than one genre in a story, complicating a reader's interpretative process, is significant for a reader because, as Peter Rabinowitz has pointed out, "genres can be seen not only the traditional way as patterns or models that writers follow in constructing texts, but also from the other direction, as different packages of rules that readers apply in construing them, as ready-made strategies for reading" (177).

"The Wide Net" builds on a generic mixing; it is a vernacular tale about a back-country couple's marital squabble that slips into the mythic tradition of the heroic quest. As she often does, Welty leads a reader to begin making meaning within the context of a "primary framework"—a term borrowed from sociologist Irving Goffman's discussion of the contextuality of interpretation (21). Then Welty guides a reader to suspect that this initial framing has been a misframing and to readjust that first interpretive strategy. The reader's reworking adds a layer to the interpretation which is still attached to the first frame and its meanings; the layers created by these multiple frameworks may subsequently interact.[2]

A reader meeting "The Wide Net" for the first time begins what appears to be a realistic short story about William Wallace Jamieson's bemused reaction to his wife Hazel's first pregnancy. This father-to-be is troubled by a feeling that he has lost Hazel to some mystery; he feels excluded and resents her acting as though she were about to deliver, although she is only three months pregnant. In response to the situation, he has slipped away to a carnival in Carthage, Mississippi, and then stayed out all night with two boys down the road. But when he returns home, he does not find a chastened, more attentive Hazel. Instead he spots a little letter announcing her intention not to put up with him, but to drown herself. In his distress, William Wallace turns for help to his friend Virgil Thompson, who has sat "on his neck" with him all the previous night, "done as much as he done, and come home at the same time" (174). Together the two organize and conduct a river-dragging party.

Students of mine sometimes say that in their first encounter with the story they loved reading "The Wide Net," but they wonder why the tone of the story eventually seems genuinely celebratory when it might be expected to be full of comic grief. They echo Virgil's question to William Wallace: "Was you out catching cotton-tails, or was you out catching your wife?" (172). It is entirely reasonable that when Hazel's husband gorges himself with fresh-caught fried fish, lapses into a sated sleep and wakes to dance with a catfish hanging from his belt, initial readers may feel startled, and either pleased or puzzled depending on their flexibility and their range of literary experience.[3]

One way to understand the tale's mid-stream generic transform-ation from a realistic tale to something else is through its allusions.

When it begins, William Wallace has, after all, just spent the night with Virgil. And like Vergil's Aeneas who wandered from his duty and his destiny in Queen Dido's Carthage, William Wallace has strayed from husbandly devotion at a carnival in Mississippi's Carthage.

Welty transforms a realistic short story into one lightly laced with the heroic epic, and then transforms the epic form that she lightly evoked. Susan Gubar has said[4] that while women writers tend to escape their strained relationships with some conventional literary forms through generic amalgamations, she found that in putting together *The Norton Anthology of Women's Literature* she had not come across a woman writing the heroic epic. But it is clear that Welty is revising that form, transforming it precisely as it is gendered.

Vergil's *Aeneid* is not a single, privileged reference that readers must find evoked by the text in order to appreciate it. Nor is it a single key allusion that all studious readers must inevitably find. Michael Kreyling, for example, is helped by memories of Dante taking Vergil as a companion in his search for Beatrice (and later of the attitude of the madonna in Hazel's final gesture) (*Eudora Welty* 19). It would be inaccurate to claim that Welty's tale recreates any one epic. Rather the story evokes the generic elements of the mythic, heroic quest. Its comic tone is in part the product of a reader's barely conscious awareness of parody and transformation.

Consider, for example, William Wallace's band of men. As if we were in a Homerian epic, we find the clans of Dover represented in it: the eight giant Malones, the Doyles and their noisy dogs, Grady and Brucie Rippen who are tied to this search by their history (their father had drowned in the Pearl River) and two black boys, Sam and Robbie Bell. These troops stomp and paw each other, eager to go, attending while their leaders apply to wise Old Doe for permission to use the wide net; Old Doc himself plays the part of oracle. He is a seer who could foretell the day's outcome, but instead he only obliquely hints at it, not quite revealing fate's decree. He waits patiently for the inevitable to come to pass, and for the order of the universe to become as clear to others as it is to him. As Ruth Vande Kieft points out (57–58), there are also the ordeals which the questing hero survives. Like Aeneas who voyaged into the underworld, William Wallace dives to the deepest spot on the Pearl River, a spot "so dark that it was no longer the muddy world of the upper river but the dark, clear world of deepness" and returns from "the gloom of such depths" with an intuition of the "true trouble that Hazel had fallen into" (180). Later he faces the inhabitant of these depths, that river creature, the King of Snakes, and he stares him down. Next he directs his men through a storm which steals the goldenness of the day. Lashing its tail "through the air," this tempest breaks the river "in a wound of silver," and fills the air with fragrance and a mystery reminiscent of Hazel's troubling mystery. Encountering this dragon-tailed storm, our hero founders on a sharp rock, opening a wound he later carries as a trophy of his quest. He reenters that town of Dover not obviously successful in his quest, but oddly triumphant.

Although the story shares several elements with the heroic epic, a reader making full sense of it must know that it also differs from them, and departs from expectations formed on knowledge of that genre. And this need to revise our expectations again, as in so many of Welty's works, brings us to the story's center. William Wallace, triumphant though he seems to be when he returns to Dover, has not in any obvious sense triumphed. That is, he has set out to find Hazel, but returns without her.

Unlike the traditional epic hero whose goal is clear, William Wallace's is not. For William Wallace needs, not to find Hazel, but to gain insight into what has possessed her and caused trouble between them. That is what Hazel, by writing her note, sends William Wallace to discover in the Pearl River. The effect of her suicide note is to send him into the natural world as it approaches its own "changing-time." And so Hazel leaves her husband to observe nature's cycle at this moment when, as Doc puts it, "any day now the change will come"

> It's going to turn from hot to cold, and we can kill the hog that's ripe and have fresh meat to eat. Come one of these nights and we can wander down here and trace a nice possum. Old Jack Frost will be pinching things up. Old Mr. Winter will be standing in the door. Hickory tree there will be yellow. Sweet-gum red, hickory yellow, dogwood red, sycamore yellow.... Magnolia and live-oak never die. Remember that. Persimmons will all get fit to eat, and nuts will be dropping like rain all through the woods here. And run, little quail, for we'll be after you too. (176)

Standing on the verge of this ordered change and then immersing himself in the Pearl River, William Wallace intuits what Hazel must feel as she prepares to give birth: "the elation that comes of great hopes and changes, sometimes simply of the harvest time, that comes with a little course of its own like a tune to run in the head" (180). That is, he rediscovers the excitement that nature's changeful cycles can generate. This is what he celebrates finding. Welty has amalgamated the pattern of heroic epic to emphasize the powerful (and mysterious) cycles of nature over a powerful hero's conquest—and made a female revision of a literary form by blending elements of comic realism, pastoral and epic. This accommodation of forms, one to the other, is appropriate to the story's content in which William Wallace comes to accommodate something female and puzzling.

Welty makes William Wallace wander into a harmony with nature that causes him to rejoice when he intended to drag the river for his wife's body. As he returns home from this odd experience, he hears the music of "the Sacred Harp Sing"—female music that seems to evoke an oblique and comic transformation of the Sirens' songs that attracted previous wanderers. William Wallace associates this celestial music permeating the woods with nature's female principle. "He [smiles] faintly, as he would at his mother, and at Hazel, and at the singing women in his life, now all one young girl standing up to sing under the trees the oldest and longest ballads there were." Then in the night sky, he sees a rainbow which looks to him "in the light of the moon ... small and of gauzy material, like a lady's summer dress, a faint veil through which the stars showed" (187). Affected by his glad knowledge of the Pearl River's depths, the night sky and the mysterious part that women play in mother nature's order, William Wallace walks back into his house. And there he finds Hazel awaiting his return from the ordeal she had conceived. Like some fairy-tale hero who has earned his heart's desire by successfully completing a series of tasks, William Wallace finds his life restored to routine domesticity. He feels relief, but also anger with Hazel who, coolly hidden in the closet, had watched him read her suicide note. Asserting himself against her mysterious and knowing superiority, he turns her upside down and spanks her. And she, responding unpredictably to his challenge, crawls into the crook of his arm. Then as she gazes into "the dark fields where the lightning bugs flickered," he stands beside her with a frown on his face, straining to see what she sees there in the natural world. And when, after a few minutes, she takes him by the hand and leads him into the house, "smiling as if she were smiling down on him" (188), a reader may feel that though William Wallace will never share Hazel's experience entirely, he may now better intuit the source and implication of her mystery.

Return then to the reader's initial notion that somehow in the course of the day William Wallace wandered from his purpose: to recover Hazel. That first impression needed revision, even though Welty appeared to confirm it in Virgil's question "was you out catching cottontails or was you out catching your wife?" As in the case of Aeneas, who to all first appearances was waylaid from his purpose and destiny in Carthage, the wandering of a hero may prove to be his destiny, the path by which he will arrive where he is going—in this case, by way of a river—dragging with the boys from the town.

Readers may not be entirely comfortable with "The Wide Net" until they consciously or, more probably, intuitively identify the genres which intertwine in it. This is not the case with *The Robber Bridegroom*, a fairy tale which evokes multiple sources and is more highly allusive than "The Wide Net." There, the tale does not discomfort the reader who neither senses nor recognizes its sources. But the reader who discovers the tale's allusiveness is rewarded when memories of fairy tale, history, legend and myth interact with the text, and that reader may find the tale considerably darker than the one who reads without these.

The list of allusions which critical readers of *The Robber Bridegroom* have compiled in their commentary is long indeed. J. A. Bryant, Jr. began a brief directory to these in his 1968 monograph, *Eudora Welty*:

> In addition to the general shape of Grimm's story, suggestions and reminiscences of a number of other tales are discoverable here, among them "The Little Goose Girl," "Rumpelstiltskin," "Little Snow White," "The Fisherman and His Wife," "Beauty and the Beast," Charles Perrault's "Cinderella," and the Hellenic myth of Cupid and Psyche. Moreover, a great deal of American folklore and near-folklore gets worked into the narrative, the stories of Davy Crockett and Mike Fink, the atrocities of Big Harpe and Little Harpe, and tall tales about Indians, frontiersmen and bandits of the Natchez Trace. (17)

Many of the allusions in this tale resemble dark threads that run through the fabric of a light, bright text. There, in the brightness where rape is obscured by the colors of love and murder, by those of marriage, these dark threads running across the story's most obvious pattern are also a part of its look. A reader's overall impression may be that the tale's fabric is colorful and celebratory, while it holds in its background the darker hues of a lament for lost innocence (the nation's as well as Rosamond's).

As a fairy tale, *The Robber Bridegroom* belongs, by Welty's own definition, to a genre that is "not innocent," but has "been to the end of experience and back" ("And They All Lived Happily"). Some readers have argued that Welty's story is too dark to be called a fairy tale,[5] underestimating Welty's respect for the dark side of the fairy tale genre and the extent to which fairy tale allusions are sometimes directly responsible for the dark coloring of Welty's tale. The fairy tale, in spite of its conventional ending, is a genre that regularly offers dramatic instruction in man's dual nature and dark side. Welty herself has described the fairy tale genre in this way:

> ogres who enjoy eating people show children very well in fantasy what will threaten them later on.... We are all brothers, but some of us are loveless. If fairy tales stir the imagination toward benevolence with the "good" fairies, they can awaken respect for the power of the "bad" fairies. Without the old fairy tales, children today could easily think malice and ill will are nothing but a set of miniature, sanitized, plastic toys—"giants 'n' ogres"—that come free in boxes of cereal at the supermarket. ("And They All Lived Happily")

If fairy tales teach that "we are all brothers, but some of us are loveless," Welty's allusions in *The Robber Bridegroom*—to Grimm's and other old tales—are designed to carry news of this potential treachery. Her echoes of fairy, tales emphasize familial lovelessness—the wife who does not love her husband, the mother who does not love her child. Her Salome, for instance, is an embodiment of the spirit of stepmotherliness. She is a composite of three characters by Grimm: the never-satisfied, husband-abusing old woman from "The Fisherman's Wife"; the unnatural mother of "Hansel and Gretel" who, because she is unwilling to share her food with her children, sends them into the forest hoping they will never return; and the jealous queen of "Little Snow White," that terrible replacement for a loving mother who demands that her stepdaughter's heart be brought to her. In Welty's retelling, Salome resembles that jealous queen as she poisons Rosamond's metaphoric heart by infecting it with suspicion. And Salome, again like the jealous stepmother in Grimm's "Snow White," pays for her crime when she is coerced to dance herself to death—a detail of Grimm's original version lost to those of us who grew up with altered retellings. But in the original, as in Welty's tale, she "had to dance until she fell down dead to the ground" (*Frog King* 190). Allusions such as these act as character, plot and motif pointers, guiding the reader to recognize quickly Welty's variations on the archetype.

Welty also spins the tale's thread of doubleness "out of the times" (*Eye* 310), that is, out of the American past. Evoking an American literary tradition, she creates the wilderness as a place of anarchic, if sometimes liberating, lawlessness and then establishes a parallel between it and the morally ambiguous settlement where greed is sated legally. She calls up American literature, legend and history to darken the tapestry of her tale. She adapts, from the narratives of those who survived capture by Indians in the seventeenth and eighteenth centuries, a setting in which to uncover man's capacity for ungodly acts. She recreates the wilderness of the Natchez Trace where little Wiley Harpe, her "Little Harp," once carried the detached head of his own brother Micajah—wanted dead or alive—in preserving, blue Mississippi mud, as if it were a bank check to be cashed when needed. Welty also adapts southwestern humor, particularly those violent yet beguiling tales that chronicle the adventures of strutting, law-defying Mike Fink, half-horse, half-alligator. Merrill Maguire Skaggs and Melody Graulich have both written on Welty's adaptation of this genre. Skaggs argues that Welty's combination of southwestern humor with the fairy tale reveals the extent to which both genres are about the use of "extravagance ... to confront basic fears and anxieties" (97) and an assertion of wished-for invulnerability. And Graulich, looking at how southwestern humor is itself a genre which breaks out of narrative conventions, discusses how Welty breaks its conventions by dropping the conventional framing narrator's voice, often used to constrain the voice of the roarer, and by allowing her narrator to speak the language of fantasy. In one especially provocative remark Graulich suggests that Welty revises the gender of this genre, creating a female tall tale in which "power comes through emotional rather than physical strength" (289), a view perhaps paralleling my reading of "The Wide Net."

These two types of allusion—to the fairy tales and to the American folklore named by Welty's various commentators and specifically cited in Welty's own essay, "Fairy Tale of the Natchez Trace"—murmur below the composition's most optimistic tones; they whisper distress. Distress, lament and the dark tones of this narrative have received much critical attention as the tale has been discussed as an American pastoral, "a putdown of mercantile probity" (French 186), a comic consideration of an historical change. Yet there is reason to give the female focus of Rosamond and her adolescent emotional discoveries centrality[6] and to emphasize three allusions which softly sound variations on the theme of the robber bridegroom. These allusions may be the most provocative of the group. For this fiction is one of Welty's many stories about a troubling love that reveals the need to transform a discovered separateness. Knowledge of these three source fictions, along with a perception of how Welty differs from these, can guide a reader's developing understanding.

First and most obvious among these sources is Grimm's "The Robber Bridegroom" (*German Popular Tales*). In that tale a young woman is engaged to, but ultimately saved from, a dangerous lover who threatens her innocence and her life. The heroine wanders into the forest one day to spy on her suitor. There she is warned by a bird and an old woman "to turn back my bonny, turn away home" (the refrain that Welty borrows). In spite of this warning the girl proceeds and discovers her betrothed, cutting other girls into pieces and salting them. A finger, chopped off for the wedding ring on it, flies into the observing girl's lap. She escapes undetected with this evidence of the danger approaching with her own wedding night. At her marriage ceremony, she produces the severed finger from her bodice, exposing her groom's violence. Then this loveless, lawless bridegroom, who is clearly associated with the sexual experience that cuts off childhood and threatens chastity, is, ultimately restrained and arrested.

Ominous potential parallels occur to the reader familiar with Grimm's terrible robber bridegroom. And although the comedy of

Welty's variant clearly promises that these predictions will be transformed, the allusion may alter the reader's perception of Jamie. For, having compared him to Grimm's bridegroom, a reader searches him for a sinister potential. And what does a reader find? Like the robber bridegroom, Jamie does away with a young girl—but by transforming her into the wife he takes. He accomplishes this when, robbing Rosamond of all her clothing, he awakens in her imagination visions of his return for "that which he ... left her ... before" (65), effectively ending her girlhood. He is not threatening as is Little Harp—the menacing double who covets Lockhart's success, then kills the girl he thinks is Jamie's and finally mounts her in sadistic conquest on a food-littered table. Harp personates the fearsome aspects of Grimm's character; rapacious, he slices off his victim's finger, and it pops into our hidden heroine's lap. But this doubling of robber bridegrooms whispers at least of a potential similarity between these two characters.

And that is the point that strikes Rosamond, although the reader who remembered Grimm may have felt it first. The severed finger, token of Harp's cruel passion, awakens in Rosamond, not only a terror of Harp, but a mistrust of her own Jamie's potential for lovelessness. In panic, she identifies so strongly with her violated double that she almost believes she is killed. This suddenly suspicious girl, daughter of Clement Musgrove, has been raised on the story of how her father's first loving mate gave way to another, selfish, jealous and insatiably greedy. Familiar with the danger of her father's spouse, Rosamond is concerned that she does not know Jamie's true identity. Perhaps the lover who comes to her wearing a mask is more robber than bridegroom.

Rosamond's fear is also underscored by allusion, overt but rarely identified,[7] to a ballad known as "Young Andrew," whose first stanzas Rosamond sings as she sits dreaming in her room and then again as she goes into the woods to meet Jamie:

> The moon shone bright, and it cast a fair light:
> "Welcome" says she, "my honey, my sweet!
> For I have loved thee these seven long year,
> And our chance it was we could never meet."
>
> Then he took her in his armes-two,
> And kissed her both cheek and chin,

And twice or thrice he kissed this may
Before they were parted in twin. (32)

Although these two stanzas are quoted in the text, the reader
benefits who knows the unsung portion of this ballad. In it, Andrew
persuades the girl who loves him to rob her father so they may marry.
But later he unpredictably steals all her clothing as well as the money she
has taken for his sake; abandoning her, he gives her the choice of going
home naked or dying on the spot. When the jilted girl is sent off by the
robber bridegroom who preferred to steal all she would have freely
given, she returns home to her father. Her father, however, sets so much
store on his gold that he leaves her to die naked on his doorstep, maimed
by two loveless men.

Again, expectations based on this source will not be fulfilled. The
ballad, like Grime's fairy tale, will be transformed rather than recreated.
But certainly the possibilities suggested by the ballad are evoked for a
purpose. Although they do not accurately foreshadow Jamie Lockhart's
behavior (since Jamie proves to be guilty of greed, but not of domestic
treachery), they serve as motif pointers in another way. Rosamond's
preoccupation with the ballad allows a reader to glimpse both her
strategy for self-creation (that is to fictionalize her way into her future) as
well as her simultaneous yearning for romantic love and suspicion of it.

Rosamond at first uses the old ballad of betrayal to conjure up a
lover (just as the ballad's heroine calls up her dream: "As I was cast in my
ffirst slepe, / A dreadful draught in my mind I drew, / Ffor I was dreamed
of a yong man, / Some men called him yonge Andrew." [*Child* 432]).
Singing aloud, she rehearses the notion of a romantic adventure and
imaginatively explores the risk of love. Jamie finds "Rosamond singing
so sweetly, as if she had been practicing just for this" (45–46). Then he
and she borrow their interchange from the ballad's storyline. Jamie's
interest in each successive layer of clothing, Rosamond's appeal "were
you born of a woman?" (48) and Jamie's reply that he will have all, as
well as Rosamond's story of the father and seven brothers who will want
revenge, and her decision to go home naked rather than die on the point
of a sword, all come from the original. In effect, when these two meet,
they invent their lives along the ballad's lines. Singing the ballad and
telling its story, Rosamond is educating herself to an idea of a potentially
dangerous sexual union which she plans to disarm. This fictional

exploration is part of the girl's education for marriage, and Welty's tale echoes Shakespearean comedies in which young men and women in forest settings educate themselves for union in plots rich in mistaken (that is, unrecognized) identities. This connection between Rosamond's singing of the ballad and her education for marriage is reinforced by Bernard Cook's discovery that in early southern Mississippi among families of means, the robber bridegroom fiction played a role in marriage ceremonies. After marriage was arranged, a ritualized abduction was enacted; the bridegroom and his party would ride on horseback to snatch the bride from her porch where she waited with her party. The ceremony, begun in ambush, would at last end in contractual vows.

On any reading it is obvious that Rosamond, filled with an adolescent eagerness for experience, is imaginatively set to turn whatever comes her way towards love. And that she—perhaps contradictorily—cannot help fearing the longed-for lover whom she cannot fully know. But the reader who misses Welty's allusion to "Young Andrew" of course does not recognize the couple's reenactment of the ballad, and so may not fully perceive Rosamond's habit of fitting her life to stories she knows. This character trait has earned her a reputation for lying, but the fictions that fall from her lips are neither snakes nor toads. They are instead the pearls of a romantic girl who lives with fantasy and reality interacting in her head. In this habit, she authors life while familiar with its literary sources and allusions, and uses her imagination (as it intersects with Jamie's) to transform robbery into love. The pessimistic expectations that a reader might base on "Young Andrew" are disappointed when Rosamond successfully recasts the melancholy ballad in a comic genre. And yet those discarded expectations are belatedly and unexpectedly fulfilled when her imagination, retaining the picture of love as separateness and vulnerability, generates suspicion and discord.[8]

The story's further development alludes to Apulieus's *The Golden Ass* and another tale that balances longing for love with the suspicion of love. There the story of Psyche and Eros is told to a frightened young woman who has dreamt of and feared being stolen from her bridal bed by a band of robbers. In the narrative told to calm and to instruct her, the young woman's fear is itself revealed to be more dangerous than the unknown lover.

In that story within a story, young Psyche is warned by her three jealous sisters that the mysterious lover who comes to her in the dark is a monster. The mortal girl allows this slander to breed suspicion. Soon she cannot overcome her apprehension. Her lover, Eros himself, warns her that he will leave her if she ever looks too closely at him. But Psyche, with her name that suggests that mind and its rationality, is unable to maintain unquestioning faith and turns a prying light onto Eros while he sleeps. When she does, a drop of her lamp's hot oil burns his shoulder, and the slumbering god of love awakens and departs. Only after arduous pursuit does Psyche regain Eros, to become his wife and a goddess.

In Welty's version, Salome[9] plays the jealous slanderer who seduces the young beloved to suspicion. Feeding Rosamond's mistrust of the masked lover who, for reasons of his own, is unwilling to reveal himself, Salome tells Rosamond:

> I fear, my dear, that you feel in your bosom a passion for a low and scandalous being, a beast who would like to let you wait on him and serve him, but will not do you the common courtesy of letting you see his face. It can only be for the reason that he is some kind of monster. (123)

Rosamond, who has attentively heard her father wonder if his loving wife and his selfish wife are not perhaps the same woman, whose beauty he loved so well at first that for a time it obliterated her ugliness, carefully attends Salome's words. She is alarmed by her ignorance of her lover and has not yet recognized that this mystery of identity has nothing to do with berry stains. When she leaves her father and stepmother and returns to Jamie's den to see Little Harp assume Jamie's place and then assault her by proxy, she is "torn as she had never been before with an anguish to know [her own lover's] name and true appearance" (134). She betrays her promise to Jamie by removing his mask, and watches him flee.

But for Rosamond, whose anxieties about betrayal, about the failure of love and about unknowable others have been released, this act of unmasking Jamie is not reassuring. And this is where Welty's tale surprises expectations based on a reader's knowledge of the Psyche/Eros story. Unlike Psyche, who finds Eros revealed beneath her lover's mask, Rosamond finds no answers in Jamie's face. Not the god of love, he is apparently robber, bridegroom and still unknown. Rosamond's unrelieved perplexity over Jamie's nature disappoints expectations based

on allusion to *The Golden Ass*. This characteristic deviation from
expectation, here as elsewhere in Welty's fiction, signals to us the scene's
thematic importance.

Rosamond has met Jamie in the wooded wilderness of her
imagination and loved him without knowing him at a time when she was
herself caught in change and eager for love. She knew him so little that
when she was reintroduced to him outside of the romantic forest, she did
not recognize him, nor did he recognize her. She could not see her dark
lover in the orthodox caller, nor could he see his beauty in the silly girl.
Their romance, perhaps nourished by their repudiation of everyday
identities, thrived on their ignorance of one another. But when they
lived together, the question of Jamie's identity plagued Rosamond. In
time she—who at first rejoiced in his successful theft of her love—grew
disturbed by her inability to name her lover. Then "she would wake up
out of her first sleep and study [Jamie's] sleeping face" only to find that
"she did not know the language it was written in."

> She would look out the window and see a cloud put up a
> mask over the secret face of the moon, and she would hear
> the pitiful cries of the night creatures. Then it was enough to
> make her afraid, as if the whole world were circled by a band
> of Indian savages, and she would shake poor Jamie until he
> shouted up out of his sleep, and rouse him to see his eyes
> come open. (84–85)

Rosamond, who has uneasily come to dread her husband's unknown
nature, does not precisely recognize what she fully feels—that her love
has not so much been a discovery of another as a self-discovery. This is
the rule rather than the exception in Welty's fictions. In "Livvie," for
example, a girl is kissed by yet another robber bridegroom, one who
steals her from a passionless marriage. Touched by him, she is "dazzled
at herself ... as he had been dazzled at himself to begin with" (236).
Sexuality awakens Rosamond, like Livvie, not to her lover but to herself.
Discoveries of sexual desire and personal identity mingle. In Welty's
fiction, love often reveals the self's particular separateness as well as a
similar quality intuited, but not exactly known, in the beloved.

Young Rosamond, however, knows little of such limitations and
will not content herself to love the mysterious Jamie who is "visible and

present" (86). She innocently feels she must know her lover's identity, which she assumes is simple and discernible, although hidden. But we readers, who know the complexity of his character more thoroughly than if he were an actual acquaintance, recognize that Jamie is not simple. He is robber and bridegroom, romantic and conventional, hero and businessman. When we first meet him, he simultaneously reveals himself as both hero and thief in the one gesture of saving Clement from Mike Fink. The fact of this doubleness is explained to Rosamond by her father, but she does not at first accept the explanation that Jamie is both bandit and lover. Only when in the course of time she removes Jamie's mask and sees for herself that faces reveal no mysteries and names untie no knots, does she, without another thought, accept the ambiguity she had resisted, only then does she decide to live with an imprecisely known, ambiguous nature, rather than live alone. She pursues the love that left her when she studied it too closely, regaining it in New Orleans, that city where "beauty and vice and every delight possible to the soul and body stood hospitably, and usually together, in every doorway" (182). And there she appropriately gives birth to Jamie's twins.

By having robbery and rape lead to fairy-tale love, Welty upsets those pessimistic expectations her reader may have built on knowledge of Grimm's "The Robber Bridegroom" and the ballad of "Young Andrew." Unlike Grimm's tale where the institution of marriage is dissolved by the threat of sexual violence, Welty's retelling seems to show lawlessness deferring to social order. The dangers discovered by Rosamond's literary predecessors seem at last resolved when her own romantic robber bridegroom kills his evil double "for the sake of [his] future and his love" (*Eye* 312). This done, the potentially predatory lover may become the prosperous husband and father of twins. Welty's fairy tale—rather than bringing news of lovelessness—seems again to be like a Shakespearean romance or a novel of manners in which lawlessness is eventually contained by a marriage contract.

But if this tale evokes older, more sinister tales only to transform them joyously, it also upsets whatever optimistic expectations may be built by allusions to *The Golden Ass*. Here fear cannot be cleared away by knowledge. The discomforting associations that are companions to this tale, the surprisingly dark contours that lurk in this coy fiction, are never wholly obliterated: For this tale about doubleness is neither simple, nor clearly optimistic. Its happily-ever-after resolution teases us, but leaves us with the problems of a love initiated by robbery and rape. And Jamie himself permits no one to ask of him what he is: a hero whose motto is "take first and ask afterward" (69) and who never alters his nature but only his appearance. If, at the story's conclusion, the bridegroom seems to part ways with the robber to become "a gentleman of the world ... respected by all" (183), the fact is that Jamie has only washed his face and called on the thief to help the merchant, "enjoying all the same success he had ever had" (184–85). He is, then, as always, the hero inextricably entwined with the robber, "with the power to look both ways and to see a thing from all sides" (185).

Add to these ambivalences their context in a fairy tale so evidently built on stories that it reminds us that robbery and rape lead to love in fiction only, not in life.[10] Welty's allusions, having intensified the reader's awareness of being immersed in fiction, undercut the robber bridegroom's transformation with the aura of make-believe, and leave us uncertain of the fiction's optimism. This fairy tale, through the emphasis it places on human complexity, adjusts the genre it adapts. For as much as Welty respects Grimm's archetypal rendering of love and lovelessness, she finds his fairy-tale promise of evil's exile inadequate to her ambiguous America where good and evil are not so distinct as fairies and ogres. In her tale, resolution is ambiguous—another appearance which is not a reality.

If in *The Robber Bridegroom* Welty retells and implicitly comments on several old tales, "At The Landing," the closing story in the collection published next, is itself a retelling of her *The Robber Bridegroom*. For Welty not only alludes to twice-told tales, but also occasionally retells stories that she has herself told before, transposing plots used once; performing them again—with a difference—in other genres. When doubles such as these are brought to Welty's attention, she often seems rather dismayed; her "did-I-do-that" tone expresses a writer's concern for originality (a concern also disclosed in responses to questions about allusions). Her tone sometimes suggests that these remarkably original and yet related tales are semiconscious variations. But story doubles— "double" here used unconventionally to suggest plots similar in situation but performed in different story genres—exist in Welty's canon and may be a mine for articles on the connectedness of her work. Pairs like "Flowers for Marjorie" and "The Wide Net"—which treat two husbands' uneasy responses to their wives' pregnancies—explore a single premise in two distinct genres. *Delta Wedding* and *Losing Battles* are another example of this sort of doubling; they each examine a family's use of story and ritual against change; the earlier fiction develops that premise in a modern novel of manners peopled with relatively sober southern gentry, while the later one, evoking the southern tall-tale tradition, develops country folk and broad comedy. *The Robber Bridegroom* and "At The Landing," written in fairly close sequence, are another interallusive pair.

The later story is the earlier tale's situational twin, but born outside of the fairy-tale genre. It too is set in and around Rodney's Landing, treats a rape received as love and its heroine is Jenny Lockhart (her last name appears on her mother's tombstone). This name—so close to Jamie Lockhart's—connects the two fictions, urging a consideration of their relationship, the patterns they share and how the later tale comments on the earlier one. This connectedness, then, is how allusion (even what may be unconscious allusion) leads a reader to create understanding "in relation to"—or in this instance, how the reader may understand "At The Landing" as not *The Robber Bridegroom*.

Jenny is another adolescent girl who, dreaming of love, is attracted to an unknown lover who rides through the woods on a red horse. And like Rosamond, Jenny has lost her mother. But unlike the fairy-tale parent who died romantically of a mother's grief when she lost her infant son, Jenny's parent more realistically died of a daughter's frustration when her father turned jailer. Raised by this severe grandfather who deprecated his daughter's raving as "a force of Nature and so beneath notice or mention" (242), young Jenny has grown within his confining restrictions and has had little enough to do with the female nature made emblematic by river water in this and other of Welty's fictions. (The river baptisms in "The Wide Net," "The Wanderers" and *Delta Wedding* all similarly emblematize an immersion to female nature.) When the story opens, the overly protective old man is himself dying. He comes to Jenny in his sleep to say that the river is rising ("It has come ...") and "made a complaint of it" (240). Anticipation of the day when she will be free to come and go trembles about her like "distant lightning" (242). She watches in the woods for a dreamt-of lover, but cannot imagine "what [is] to come" (244) until, like Rosamond when she sang "Young Andrew," Jenny conceives of separateness. Rosamond recognizes this potential source of pain from her father's stories and her favorite ballad.

But Jenny perceives separateness in an observation of the life around her. Seeing Mag, she conceives of love, separateness and the possibility that these lie in store for her, too.

Once noticed, the counterpoint of similarity and difference between the two stories is obvious. When high water comes—with its overtones of passion, birth and baptism inextricably bound with change, danger and death—Floyd saves Jenny. Then when her eyes are "clear upon him, [he violates] her" (251). Like Rosamond, Jenny has longed for the violation of her isolation, and she attempts to use the power of her imagination to create love. But like the girl in "A Memory," Jenny invents a love that is challenged by Floyd's actual presence.

> If she could have followed and found him then, she would have started on foot. But she knew what she would find when she would come to him. She would find him equally real with herself—and could not touch him then. As she was living and inviolate, so of course was he, and when that gave him delight, how could she bring a question to him? ... Nothing in Floyd frightened her that drew her near, but at once she had the knowledge come to her that a fragile mystery was in everyone and in herself, since it was there in Floyd, and that whatever she did, she would be bound to ride over and hurt, and the secrecy of life was the terror of it. (245)

Intuiting without fully knowing Floyd's otherness, and projecting onto Floyd the vulnerable position his separateness creates for her (as the girl of "A Memory" did as she "speculated endlessly on the dangers" [76] of her class-mate's home), Jenny hesitates to touch Floyd, fearing to find "him equally real with herself." She is drawn to something mythic rather than real in Floyd, who is for her—as Brookhart and Marts have pointed out—"charged with the river country's vitality and mystery" (89). For Jenny, Floyd is a mythic wanderer who counterpoints her confinement. For her as for a Welty reader who is rereading or reading out of chronological sequence, Billy Floyd is as much an Aengus figure as King MacLain, and "At The Landing" may evoke *The Golden Apples* as well as *The Robber Bridegroom*. "In the long shadows," Floyd's figure appears with "the gleaming fish" (243)—an emblem of longing and desire whose name Jenny calls. But when Floyd finally grasps Jenny, she is taken not by the longed-for mythic lover, but by a wandering and dangerous beloved who "lived apart in delight" and about whom she has glimpsed something "used and worldly." Welty humorously underlines Floyd's doubleness when she juxtaposes Jenny's thought in the story before the flood that "there was something handled and used about Floyd, strong as an odor" (248), with the postmaster's comment aloud on flood slime.

Jenny Lockhart's encounter with Floyd echoes Rosamond's with Jamie Lockhart, but the contrast between Jenny who from her story's outset is confined in imagery of enclosure and Rosamond who roams outdoors, is critical.

> For all her life the shy Jenny could look, if she stayed in the parlor, back and forth between her mother's two paintings, "The Bird Fair" and "The Massacre at Fort Rosalie." Or if she went in the dining room she could walk around the table or sit on one after the other of eight needlepoint pieces, each slightly different, which her mother had worked and sewn to the chairs, or she could count the plates that stood on their rims in the closet. In the library she could circle an entirely bare floor and make up a dance to a song she made up, all silently, or gaze at the backs of the books without titles— books that had been on ships and in oxcarts and through fire and water, and were singed and bleached and swollen and shrunken, and arranged up high and nearly unreachable, like objects of beauty. (241)

Jenny is circumscribed by indoor spaces and limiting images, and then described with the language of passivity and obedience:

> Jenny was obedient to her grandfather and would have been obedient to anybody, to a stranger in the street if there could be one. She never performed any act, even a small act, for herself, she would not touch the prisms. It might seem that nothing began in her own heart. (242–43)

In the house she lives an object among objects, enclosed and protected as they are. She can be called to obedience even by her grandfather's "little murmur" (242), and yet her stillness initially contains an unsurrender paralleling "the stillness and unsurrender of the still and unsurrendering world" (243) before the flood. She contains longings that resemble the prisms with which she is associated,[11] prisms reflecting a trapped elusive light, glimmering, but not reached for. The image of her relationship to these prisms is promising but passive; Jenny hears their music, sees their color, but fears reaching to touch them.

> They gave off the faintest of musical notes when air stirred in
> any room or when only herself passed by, and they touched.
> It was her way not to touch them herself, but to let the touch
> be magical, a stir of the curtain by the outer air, that would
> also make them rainbows. (241)

Her attraction to these prisms implicitly resembles her attraction to Floyd, for whom she also fears to reach. There is, however, a contrast between the magical touch of the prisms—creating a faint music—and Floyd's touching of her—creating a slowly building cacophony.

The very heart of the contrast between Rosamond and Jenny is in their voices. Rosamond has the power to sing aloud, to retell old stories, to make them hers in ways she wishes, reshaping them to yield her story. From Rosamond's mouth, adventurous, authoritative lies fall "like diamonds and pearls" (39) while Jenny's is marked with silence. Jenny composes and sings a song "all silently." When she and Floyd walk together they hold berries in their mouths, not words. Jenny hardly speaks in this tale; her infrequent speech is characteristically reported. She only has three brief direct speeches, first to say "wake up, Grandpa" (240), next to say "go back" (244) to Floyd in an early encounter and lastly to deny the accusation that she has been, offensively silent: "I speak to you, Mag" (254). In the landing store, others pointedly speak to her in a conversational "exchange," but she does not respond. We are told that she knew she was not supposed to speak, and that eventually "in a kind of haste she whispered to the five old men" (249) of her grandfather's death. At a critical moment she is reported to have said Billy Floyd's name. Later she is not able to speak to Floyd.

> "I ..." she began, and stopped....
> She would like to tell him some strange and beautiful thing,

if she could speak at all, something to make him speak. Communication would be telling something that is all new, so as to have more of the new told back. The dream of that held her spellbound ... (251)

After "he violated her," Jenny attempts what the fairy-tale Rosamond comes closer to achieving: she attempts to transform the violation of her separateness with a story of love. Jenny's violation is as ambiguous as the flood that Floyd's name suggests, at once life's rush and violence. (This is the story of living "At The Landing"—that is, of living on high ground, out of life's water, until that water rises dangerously; the title, "At The Landing," and the town's name, "The Landing," suggest being caught on high ground rather than saved by it.) But unlike Rosamond's fairy-tale "rape," Jenny's violation indeed turns out to be rape. When Jenny attempts to speak and so to shape her story as Rosamond does by bringing her ballad to life, Jenny whispers over the sound of the lapping water. "Her words came a little louder and in shyness she changed them from words of love to words of wishing.... 'I wish you and I could be far way. I wish for a little house'" (251). But to communicate her desire to her mythic wanderer might be to confine him; she has already uncomfortably imagined him "caught and cornered in a little store," "trapped in the confined space with her between him and the door" (248). So Jenny does not speak too loudly and Floyd does not look around: "ideas of any different thing from what was in his circle of fire might never have reached his ears, for all the attention he paid to her remarks" (251). Unlike Rosamond's, Jenny's hesitant words have no transforming powers.

When Jamie Lockhart leaves Rosamond in the woods, that heroine goes home and scours her house until she is ragged and dirty. Having in that manner ordered her thoughts, she soon sets out after her lover. When in time she recognizes his nature as more complex and less perfect than she had pictured, she nevertheless claims him as he is. Jenny, when Floyd leaves her, also returns home to obsessively clean house and to put her feelings in place. Unlike Rosamond, however, Jenny hides, feeling troubled by beauty and ugliness alike because she is unwilling to discover the closeness of the two in Floyd. Her eventual response to this "shock of love" (253) is to shut down like a house with all its rooms darkened. The narrator tells us that to help her "someone would have to go slowly from room to room, slowly and darkly, leaving each one lighted behind, before going to the next" (254). Damaged, darkened and yet without having admitted Floyd's double nature, Jenny sets out to follow him because she is unable to make "any way alone" (256). Jenny wonders:

> what more love would be like. Then of course she knew. More love would be quiet. She would never be so quiet as she wished until she was quiet with her love.... It had been enough to make her desperate in her heart, the long search for Billy Floyd to give quiet to. (255)

When Jenny wanders among the fishermen asking for her lover, they are not concerned for her love, but put her inside a grounded boathouse. One by one they come in to rape her:

> she called out; she did not call any name; it was a cry with a rising sound, as if she said "Go back," or asked a question, and then at the last protested. A rude laugh covered her cry, and somehow both the harsh sounds could easily have been heard as rejoicing, going out over the river in the dark night. (258)

Jenny's final cry is an inarticulate echo of her first words to Floyd, "go back," and her long silence is overwhelmed at the story's conclusion by the boatman's callous laughter. Their rude noise, shades distinct from a joyful noise, again conveys the ambiguity of Jenny's experience with Floyd, a missed celebration. Unlike Rosamond, Jenny does not unmask emotional violence to recognize it as a real danger that she can nonetheless manage in a world where she had hoped to escape guardedness. Unfortunately the world that Jenny's grandfather had wanted her to fear and to withdraw from, proves to be worthy of fear. With no defenses other than evasion, Jenny can only extinguish all the lights in the house of her mind and hope the threat at its door will go away. In this state, Jenny "waits for Billy Floyd," her face hung with a smile "no matter what was done to her, like a bit of color that kindles in the sky after the light has gone" (258). Where Rosamond, who exists in a fairy-tale universe, can transform violation into deliverance, Jenny is overcome by the story of love with which she tries to shape experience. And she is silenced. The sound that readers are left with is not Rosamond's voice assuring her father that her story as she now authoritatively tells it, "is the truth" and not a lie ("all true but the blue canopy") (184). It is instead the inhumanly inarticulate "dull *pit*" (258) of boys' knives thrown at a tree, the sound of casual, unconcerned violence.

The Robber Bridegroom and "At The Landing," then, are variations written in the same time period. *The Robber Bridegroom* saw earlier publication, but "At The Landing" grew from a draft called "The Children" and dated 1934.[12] The two finished fictions significantly evoke one another in ways that emphasize difference. Welty has repeatedly worked toward this pattern with allusion, using it not only for the sake of building accurate character, plot or motif predictors, but for establishing expectations that need adjustment and revision. As she leads readers to consider the difference between a literary memory and the fiction-at-hand, she pushes them toward a discovery of meaning. Her use of allusion does not create correspondence so much as transformation, which habitually restructures the intentions of the source fictions, causing the reader to revise initial predictions based on the allusion.

NOTES

1. Here I am thinking of insightful works that nevertheless fit a category Welty commented on by saying, "Anyone who attributes my stories to myths very specifically and thoroughly is overshooting it. I would rather suggest things" (Gretlund 203).

2. See Dawn Kendig's article for another application of Goffman to Welty.

3. Having noticed this response in readers, I was interested to see that the made-for-television version of *The Wide Net* offered an interpretive performance of William Wallace's catfish dance that was wild-with-grief. This interpretation is not, I think, true to the text, but to initial expectations that the text moves beyond.

4. In a keynote address for "Women, Society, and The Arts," Susquehanna University, 3 November 1989.

5. Kreyling, for one, citing folklorist Francis Lee Utley, argues that "this novel is properly a 'local legend' and not simply a 'fairy tale' because it has 'a cruelty and a directness .... glossed over in the fairy tale'" ("Clement" 33).

Marilyn Arnold is another who argues that Welty's tale is in conflict with "the shallowness of the fairy tale vision" (16). Arnold, however, shrewdly suggests the role that generic allusion may play in the reader's construction of the text, stating that *Welty creates standard expectations in the reader, but she does not fulfill them. Instead, she subverts, reverses, burlesques, and just generally scatters asunder* the fairy tale's sacrosanct notions about the agenda for happily-ever-after living" (16).

6. Those who have given Rosamond rather more emphasis include Skaggs and Graulich. Skaggs's article extends Bruno Bettelheim's notions that fairy tales provide "a cultural escape valve" and that "the most important ingredient of all fairy tales is the promise of success," to the genre of southwestern humor and to Welty's tale. In making this extension, Skaggs tends to brighten Rosamond's story, suggesting that her happy ending transforms the anxieties suggested by the older plots of Grimm, Psyche and Eros or frontier humor—a conclusion with which I cannot agree entirely.

7. "Young Andrew" appears as ballad no. 48 in Francis James Child's *The English and Scottish Popular Ballads*. vol. 1. New York: Houghton, 1904. Gordon E. Sleuthang (in "Initiation in Eudora Welty's *The Robber Bridegroom*." *Southern Humanities Review* 7 [Winter 1973]: 77–78) is the only other critic I know who discusses Welty's use of this ballad.

8. The education which stories can provide is also a subject of Welty's autobiographical essay, "The Little Store." In it she remembers the moment when her own developing imagination, made bold by the news of "some act of violence" concerning the people who ran the neighborhood grocery store, strayed beyond her family's supervision.

9. Salome's name refers us to the Biblical character who traded a dance for the decapitated head of "the only man [she] ever loved" (this line from Oscar Wilde's version), a girl simultaneously awakened to sexuality and to a dangerously evil willfulness. The name strikes another allusive note.

10. As Rabinowitz points out in his discussion of narrative conventions, "undermining a conventional ending tends to stress the conventionality of that closure" (162–63), emphasizing the fictionality of that closure.

11. Is it coincidence that in *The Robber Bridegroom* "the *prism* light of day" diverts a redbird into his old song just before Jamie Lockhart rides up to rob Rosamond "of that which he had left her the day before" (63)?

12. Brookhart and Marrs discuss the development in their essay, "More Notes on River Country."

Works Cited

Apulieus, Lucius. *The Golden Ass*. New York: Marvin, 1931.

Arnold, Marilyn. "Eudora Welty's Parody." *Notes on Mississippi Writers* 2 (Spring 1978): 15–22.

Brookhart, Mary Hughes, and Suzanne Marrs. "More Notes on River Country." *Welty: A Life in Literature*. Ed. Albert J. Devlin. Jackson: UP of Mississippi, 1987. 82–95.

Bryant, J.A. *Eudora Welty*. Minnesota Pamphlet No. 66. Minneapolis: U of Minnesota P, 1968.

Child, James Francis. *The English and Scottish Popular Ballads*. vol. 1. New York: Houghton, 1904.

Cook, Bernard. "Ritual Abduction in Early Mississippi." *Mississippi Quarterly* 36.1 (1982–83): 72–73.

French, Warren. "'All Things Are Double': Eudora Welty as a Civilized Writer." *Eudora Welty: Critical Essays*. Jackson: UP of Mississippi, 1983. 77–87.

Goffman, Irving. *Frame Analysis*. New York: Harper Colophon, 1974.

Graulich, Melody. "Pioneering the Imagination: Eudora Welty's *The Robber Bridegroom*." *Women and Western American Literature*. Ed. Helen Winter Stauffer and Susan J. Rosowski. Troy, NY: Whitson, 1982. 283–96.

Gretlund, Jan Nordby. "An Interview with Eudora Welty." *Southern Humanities Review* 14 (Summer 1980): 193–208.

Grimm, Jacob, and Wilhelm Grimm. "Little Snow White." *The Frog King and Other Tales of the Brothers Grimm*. New York: New American Library, 1964.

Grimm, Jacob Ludwig Karl. *German Popular Tales*. Philadelphia: Porter, 1869.

Gubar, Susan. Keynote address at "Women, Society, and the Arts." Susquehanna U, Selinsgrove, PA. Nov. 1989.

Hirsch, E. D. *Validity in Interpretation*. New Haven: Yale UP, 1967.

Kendig, Daun. "Realities in Sir Rabbit: A Frame Analysis." *Eudora Welty: Eye of the Storyteller*. Ed. Dawn Trouard. Kent, OH: Kent State UP, 1989. 119–32.

Kreyling, Michael. *Eudora Welty: The Achievement of Order*. Baton Rouge: U of Louisiana P, 1980.

———. "Clement and the Indians: Pastoral and History in *The Robber Bridegroom*." *Eudora Welty: A Form of Thanks*. Jackson: UP of Mississippi, 1979. 25–45.

Porat, Ziva Ben. "The Poetics of Literary Allusion." *PTL: A Journal* 1 (1976): 105–28.

Rabinowitz, Peter. *Before Reading: Narrative Conventions and the Politics of Interpretation*. Ithaca: Cornell UP, 1987.

Skaggs, Merrill Maguire. "The Uses of Enchantment in Frontier Humor and *The Robber Bridegroom*." *Studies in American Humor* 3 (Oct. 1976): 96–102.

Vande Kieft, Ruth M. *Eudora Welty*. Rev. ed. Boston: Twayne, 1987.

Welty, Eudora. "And They Lived Happily Ever After." *New York Times Book Review*. Part II. 10 Nov. 1963: 3.

——. "At The Landing." *Collected Stories*. 240–58.

——. *The Collected Stories of Eudora Welty*. New York: Harcourt, 1982.

——. *The Eye of the Story*. New York: Random, 1977.

——. "Livvie." *Collected Stories*. 228–39.

——. "A Memory." *Collected Stories*. 75–80.

——. *One Time, One Place*. New York: Random, 1971.

——. *The Robber Bridegroom*. New York: Harcourt, 1942.

——. "The Wide Net." *Collected Stories*. 169–88.

Yeats, William Butler. *Selected Poems and Two Plays of William Butler Yeats*. Ed. M. L. Rosenthal. New York: Collier, 1962.

SUZANNE MARRS

"The Huge Fateful Stage of the Outside World": Eudora Welty's Life in Politics

Stories written by the imagination for the imagination. Language ranging from the highly metaphoric to the taut and spare, from the lushly descriptive to the ungrammatically conversational. Plots conveying the mystery or wildness inherent in human experience. Characters, rich and poor, educated and uneducated, black and white, who share the author's respect and sympathy and who possess the complex, contradictory natures of actual people. The person who writes such a fiction is not likely to become a political activist, is not likely to accept political set speeches that undervalue the intellect of the electorate, to accept the stereotyping and even character assassination typical of political campaigns. Such a writer is Eudora Welty, and such scruples are certainly hers, yet Welty has from the start been absolutely aware of the importance of making political decisions, of voting for those candidates most likely to support the values she holds dear, and of acting in support of causes she esteems.

Throughout her life Welty has been interested in the political process—in the candidates who run for office, in the programs they espouse, in the methods they use to win or lose elections. She has never been a neutral party in this process—a lifelong Democrat, Welty has supported Democratic candidates and liberal causes from the beginning. But in the 1930s and 1940s, Welty's Democratic Party loyalties were

From *Eudora Welty and Politics: Did the Writer Crusade?*, edited by Harriet Pollack and Suzanne Marrs. 69–87. © 2001 by Louisiana University Press. Reprinted by permission.

divided. She was appalled by Mississippi's election of demagogues like Theodore Bilbo and John Rankin even as she rejoiced in the victories of Franklin Delano Roosevelt and Harry S. Truman. Of course, only rarely did Welty give public voice to these views. More typically she expressed them privately to friends and implicitly in her stories: In 1934, she was proud to see her friend Hubert Creekmore's anti-Bilbo letter published in *Time* magazine. In 1938, her story "The Whistle" indicted the evils of a tenant-farming system and in doing so suggested the importance of programs like the Farm Security Administration's Tenant Purchase Program. And in 1948 in a letter to her friend John Robinson, she celebrated Truman's victory over Dewey and the racist Dixiecrats as the "nearest to liberal choice."[1]

Welty, however, did not always keep private the expression of her political views. A notable exception is her December 20, 1945, letter to the *Jackson Clarion-Ledger*, complaining about the paper's coverage of Gerald L. K. Smith's visit to Jackson. Smith, who had been a devout disciple of Huey Long, in 1945 proclaimed himself opposed not only to "Stalinism," but also to "Internationalism and other forms of alienism" and sought to establish the basis for a Nationalist movement in the South. Knowing that Smith was, to use the words of Walter Goodman, "the country's noisiest anti-Semite," a man who had praised Hitler, had blamed Jews for the Great Depression and World War II, and had denied the reality of the Holocaust, Welty was offended by the newspaper's nonjudgmental coverage of Smith's speech. Recognizing the legacy of Nazism and the spirit that would eventually be called McCarthyism, Welty asked the editor, "Isn't there anybody ready with words for telling Smith that that smells to heaven to us, that we don't want him, won't let him try organizing any of his fascistic doings in our borders, and to get out and stay out of Mississippi?" She went on to ask, "[I]s there still nothing we can do to atone for our apathy and out blindness or our closed minds, by maintaining some kind of vigilance in keeping Gerald Smith away?"[2]

Welty concluded her letter by denouncing Smith's ideological pals: "we will get Bilbo and Rankin out when their time, election time, comes, God willing." Well might she have called for the defeat of Mississippi politicians Theodore Bilbo and John Rankin. Indeed, both represented values that were anathema to her. Elected to the United States Senate in 1934, Bilbo sought "to send blacks 'back to Africa,'" opposed antilynching and anti-poll tax bills, and spent much of his energy preaching race hatred and white supremacy." In a stump speech during his 1946 campaign, Bilbo was in rare form: "Do not let a single nigger vote. If you let a few register and vote this year, next year there will be twice as many, and the first thing you know the whole thing will be out of hand." Attitudes like Bilbo's were especially shocking in the wake of a war ostensibly fought against Nazi Aryanism. Equally repugnant to Welty were the policies of Congressman Rankin. Rankin, who served in the House of Representatives from 1921 until 1952, was a rabble-rousing member of the House Un-American Activities Committee. An anti-Semite in the Gerald Smith mode, Rankin taunted his Jewish colleagues in the House, equating them with Communists. In addition, he sought to block Chinese immigration into the United States and opposed any political measures that might move African Americans toward equality. When the American Red Cross sought to cease labeling blood as "black" or "white," Rankin exploded this idea, he contended, was put forth by the "crackpots, the Communists and parlor pinks ... [in order] to mongrelize the nation."[3] Welty must have cringed at such comments, comments that denied the validity of the American war effort. Her public call for the defeat of Bilbo and Rankin is testimony to her extreme disgust with their values. In her hometown newspaper, the usually circumspect Welty thus made a forceful and impassioned political statement, a statement for openness, tolerance, and freedom, both of speech and of belief.

This public statement of 1945 prefigured Welty's active participation in the presidential election of 1952, a participation not in spite of her stance as fiction writer, but because of it. In New York City in the fall of 1952, she canvassed for Adlai Stevenson and sold tickets for Stevenson fund raisers, returning home in time to vote for the Democratic candidate. For Welty this was a moment of convergence; Stevenson brought to the public stage the very values that animated her fiction. She admired his forthright nature, his acceptance of diversity, his keen intellect and complexity of thought, and his use of the English language. As a result, Welty for the first and only time in her life actively joined a political campaign.

The defeat of Stevenson was a bitter pill, but her loyalty to the candidate and her hope that he might one day lead the country were unquenched. She expressed that loyalty openly one more time, this time in print when the *New Republic* requested that she and other writers send New Year's greetings to Governor Stevenson. In her message, Welty told the governor that in his campaign his supporters saw "their chiefest inner convictions translated for the time being to the huge fateful stage of the outside world" and that Stevenson "had got up and represented those convictions and brought them to bear on the scene, life-size and first-hand." In writing about inner conviction translated to the huge fateful stage of the outside world, Welty might well be describing her own attempts in fiction. In *One Writer's Beginnings*, she notes that "the outside world is the vital component of my inner life. My work, in the terms in which I see it, is as clearly matched to the world as its secret sharer. My imagination takes its strength and guides its direction from what I see and hear and learn and feel and remember of my living world."[4] This "charged dramatic field of fiction" converged with the huge fateful stage of the outside world in the election of 1952 so that Eudora Welty supported a candidate she characterized in her New Year's greeting as having "intelligence ... charged to communicate, ... shaped in responsibility and impelled with learning and curiosity, [and] ... alight with imagination." Stevenson, Welty saw, was concerned with communication and alight with imagination, and such concern and such imagination, she felt, made not merely for great literature, but also for credible political leaders, for effective political communication, and for innovative political policies.

Stevenson, as Welty recognized and admired, possessed the courage of his convictions, and during the campaign his convictions had led him to challenge directly and forcefully demands for the suppression of dissent or for partisan advantage. As David Halberstam reported, Stevenson "went before the American Legion, a citadel of jingoism and political reaction, and told the audience that McCarthy's kind of patriotism was a disgrace." The American Legion was not alone in hearing such frank comments. Stevenson biographer Jean Baker observes:

> In his childhood Adlai Stevenson had learned the virtues of self-criticism, and so throughout the campaign he offered the language of business to labor, remarking that "goons and violence and property damage are as wrong and as intolerable in labor disputes as anywhere else." In New

Haven he promised an audience of loyal party men that he would support only worthy Democratic candidates. In New Orleans he spoke on civil rights and tidelands oil. At a town hall luncheon in Los Angeles, he informed party activists that the people got the kind of leaders they deserved. "Your public servants serve you right; indeed they often serve you better than your apathy and indifference deserve."

Stevenson was a rare candidate who sought to challenge his listeners, not pander to them. That such a candidate went down in defeat raised for Welty a crucial question: "how soon and how fully can we accommodate greatness—honor it, not punish it, because it is greatness," she asked.[5]

For Welty, Stevenson's greatness lay in his recognition that political situations were too complex for simplistic answers. For example, the war in Korea was central in the mind of the electorate in 1952, but Stevenson offered no easy answers for this problem. A speech he gave in Louisville, Kentucky, is typical. There, as Baker reports, "he offered his special brand of the politics of unresolved modern dilemmas: 'I promise no easy solutions, no relief from burdens and anxieties, for to do this would be not only dishonest; it would be to attack the foundations of our greatness.' It was typical of Stevenson that he carefully and thoughtfully dissected the Korean War—its history, its manipulation by the Soviets (this was an era in which Americans misunderstood the tensions among Communist countries and exaggerated the power of the Soviets), and its necessary resolution by military containment under the United Nations." Stevenson's discussion of the multifaceted and perhaps impenetrable nature of reality held vital appeal for Welty, whose character Virgie Rainey knew that "all the opposites on earth were close together" and who herself would later write: "Relationship *is* a pervading and changing mystery.... Brutal or lovely, the mystery waits for people wherever they go, whatever extreme they run to."[6]

Finally, Stevenson's love of language, of its imaginative and precise use, set the note of the campaign in which Welty had so ardently participated. According to Baker, Stevenson paid more attention to the written text of his speeches than to their effective delivery. When his advisers argued that his defects as an orator limited his appeal to voters,

"Stevenson's reaction was expectable: 'If they don't like me as I am, *tant pis*! I won't pretend to be anything else.'" Concern for language defined Stevenson. As Baker notes, "Intent on creating carefully crafted political essays graced with complex vocabulary—the language of the university, the Washington-based institutes, and the nation's best writers ..., Stevenson paid no attention to the important consideration of advancing himself as a future president. Always the presentation of his words was secondary to the words themselves."[7] Such a stance clearly made Stevenson a writer's candidate.

If public and private thus converged for Welty in the campaign of 1952, if the fiction writer found her most interior values being championed on the "huge fateful stage of the outside world," she herself championed those values on a somewhat smaller Mississippi stage in the 1960s. That stage was literally located in the Christian Center of Millsaps College, and there Eudora Welty on April 18, 1963; and December 2, 1964, made powerful yet complex statements in favor of civil rights.

When Welty came to the podium in 1963, she came with a background of interracial relationships more diverse, extensive, and empathetic than most white Mississippians possessed. During her student days at Columbia University and later during visits to New York City, Welty had often gone to Harlem: she loved to hear jazz, played at the Cotton Club and Small's Paradise, and she had been thrilled to see an African American production of *Macbeth* directed by a young Orson Welles. In Jackson, Welty had frequented music stores in the black business district so that she could buy what were called "race records," and she had moved easily in and out of black neighborhoods, homes, and churches, photographing many a black Mississippian. Sometime in the 1940s, her editor John Woodburn introduced Welty to Ralph Ellison and took her to dinner at the Ellisons' New York apartment. It was her first social contact with African Americans, and she and Ellison became friends.[8]

Moreover, late in the 1950s Welty, often in the company of Millsaps history professor Ross Moore and his wife, began to attend events at Tougaloo Southern Christian College, an African American institution just north of Jackson. She also gave at least two lecture/readings there, one of which was sponsored by the Social Sciences Forum. According to John Quincy Adams, Tougaloo's

Professor Ernst Borinski had designed the forum as part of an effort to provide a "model of an integrated society," and Millsaps professors of history, sociology, and political science had been frequent speakers. The invitation for Welty to speak about her work was a very unusual one for the Social Sciences Forum—her fiction and her creative process had little to do with the social sciences—but simply by addressing the group Welty was issuing an implicit call for integration. In fact, the lecture came only five months after a 1958 furor about the Millsaps College Religious Forum, which had dared to invite integrationists to speak, and her lecture seems almost to have been a response to the clamor raised by local newspapers, a clamor that had prompted Millsaps to close its public events to African Americans and to discourage its professors from teaching or speaking at Tougaloo. Welty clearly regretted that Millsaps would no longer provide a "model of an integrated society," but she participated in such a model at Tougaloo, even though speaking at Tougaloo, involved some personal danger. By 1958, white visitors to Tougaloo might have expected to have their visits monitored by the State Sovereignty Commission or its informers. Welty's friend Jane Reid Petty recalls that she and others often carpooled when going to Tougaloo, varying the car they took as often as possible so that the sheriff, whom they suspected of recording the tag numbers of white visitors to Tougaloo, would not see a pattern in their visits. Though the possibility of harassment loomed in the offing, neither Welty nor her friends were deterred from this activity.[9]

Despite a history of refusing to capitulate to racist pressure, Welty must have been keenly aware that her April 18, 1963, appearance at Millsaps occurred at a particularly tense moment in the history of both the state and the college. In the fall of 1962, there had been riots and two deaths at the University of Mississippi when James Meredith had arrived to enroll. In December a black boycott of downtown Jackson stores had begun and would be the source of much hostility for more than six months. In January 1963, twenty-eight young white Methodist ministers caused outrage in the white community when they published a "*Born of Conviction* statement ..., in which they asked for a free and open pulpit in the racial crisis and full support of the public schools instead of the private schools that were being established to; maintain segregation."[10]

At Millsaps there was tension as well. Both faculty and administration overwhelmingly supported efforts for integration, but the administration in particular feared both violence and the loss of its financial base if integration came to the school. Nevertheless, on January 24, 1963, the Millsaps faculty voted 36–22–1 to support the twenty-eight Methodist ministers who had signed the *Born of Conviction* statement. The Millsaps resolution read, in part: "We are concerned ... that encroachments upon the liberties of ministers to speak freely their sincere interpretations of the Christian gospel constitute but one manifestation of those evil tendencies which would deny men freedom in every sphere. Such tendencies are a constant threat, not only to a free and valid church, but also to a democratic society." Nor was this the end of consternation felt by Millsaps faculty over the racial situation in Mississippi. On April 2, 1963, a professor and several African American students from Tougaloo College were turned away from a play at Millsaps, and on April 11, the Millsaps AAUP chapter passed another controversial resolution, this time asking the college president to appoint a committee to study the possibility of integrating the Millsaps student body.[11] A week later, it was time for the college to host the Southern Literary Festival, which was directed by Millsaps English professor and Welty friend George Boyd, one of the signers of the AAUP resolution. The college thus faced a dilemma—whether to abide by its policy of segregation, so recently enforced, or to allow open admission to Eudora Welty's April 18 address because it was sponsored by the Southern Literary Festival rather than Millsaps.

Early on that day, officials from Millsaps called upon Welty to discuss the prospect of an integrated audience—they feared conflict. Welty, nevertheless, asked that her lecture be open to all, and it was. That lecture, published almost a year earlier under the title "Words into Fiction," seems detached from any sort of political situation. In it, Welty acknowledges that a reader may have a conception of a novel that differs from that of the writer, but she contends that this difference "is neither so strange nor so important as the vital fact that a connection has been made between them." The novel, she argues, is "made by the imagination for the imagination." After delivering this address, however, Welty went on to show her audience the political import a work made by the imagination for the imagination could have—she read her story "Powerhouse" to the interracial audience, which included a contingent from Tougaloo Southern Christian College.[12]

Written in 1940 and inspired by a Fats Waller concert Welty had attended, "Powerhouse" is the story of an African American pianist and his band playing at a segregated dance; it focuses on the white audience's simultaneous fascination with and repulsion by the band leader, Powerhouse, and on the band's ability to find intermission conviviality and refreshments only at a black café. In reading this story at the festival, Welty took a considerable risk. "The point of view of this story," she has noted, "is floating around somewhere in the concert hall—it belongs to the 'we' of the audience," and that audience is a racist audience. Powerhouse, on the other hand, is drawn from Welty's own experience as a writer. Welty has said that she is driven by "the love of her art and the love of giving it, the desire to give it until there is no more left," and Powerhouse is a performer who "gives everything."[13] Thus the narrative voice located in the story's white racist audience might have offended black listeners at Millsaps even as the author's clear identification of Powerhouse as representative of artists like herself might have offended whites. But Welty trusted in the ability of her listeners, and she might well have expected the story to bring together the two factions attending the lecture and reading.

In "Powerhouse," Welty suggests that a shared act of imagination can bridge, if only momentarily, the separateness between individuals. Though neither the whites at their dance nor the black citizens Powerhouse encounters at the World Café in Negrotown consciously recognize themselves in his lyrics or tall tales, this "inspired" musician, this "fanatic," gives his white audience "the only time for hallucination" and leaves his black audience in a "breathless ring." At the dance he sends "everybody into oblivion" and at the World Café everybody "in the room moans with pleasure." The song that closes the story seems particularly relevant to this issue of communication and imagination. "Somebody loves me," Powerhouse sings and then concludes, "Maybe it's you!" Maybe, just maybe, Powerhouse will have a deep and lasting effect upon a member of his audience—the probability seems slight. Still, the story's very existence suggests that it is possible for a shared act of imagination to extend beyond the moment of performance. A Fats Waller Jackson concert, made by the imagination for the imagination, brought forth a complex, enduring, and imaginative response from Eudora Welty, a young white woman living in the Deep South.[14]

More than twenty years after writing this story based on the Waller concert, Welty read it to her 1963 Millsaps audience, black and

white, as if to proclaim the destructiveness of segregation and the
enriching effect of imagining oneself into other and different lives.
Combining her story with a lecture about the power of the imagination
to unite reader and writer was a political act for Welty, an act of courage
and vision, an act that built upon the integrated readings she had earlier
given at Tougaloo College. And Welty's presentation at Millsaps did
unite, however briefly, black and white Mississippians. John Salter, the
professor who led the Tougaloo contingent on April 18, reported,
"Eudora Welty gave an excellent lecture, including a reading of one of
her short stories—which we could follow as she read since we had
brought along several copies of her work. When the evening was over we
walked slowly outside. A group of Millsaps students came up and
indicated that they were quite glad that we had attended. Other than
that, no one appeared to notice us, and that, in its own small way, marked
a significant breakthrough in Mississippi." Welty's part in this
breakthrough won her the enduring respect of Tougaloo chaplain Edwin
King, who attended the event along with Salter and black students from
Tougaloo, and of Anne Moody, one of those black students, who in a
February 1985 appearance at Millsaps recalled how important it had
been for her to hear Welty read.[15] Nevertheless, despite Welty's actions
in support of integration and despite the standing ovation she received
from blacks and whites at the festival, Millsaps College would less than
one month later turn away African Americans who sought admission to
a theatrical production by the Millsaps Players.

Off the Millsaps campus, infinitely more virulent acts of racism
soon occurred. On May 28, a faculty member and some students from
Tougaloo were beaten and one student arrested when they attempted to
integrate the lunch counter at Woolworth's variety store. On June 12,
Medgar Evers, field secretary of the Mississippi NAACP, was
assassinated. And on June 18, John Salter and Edwin King, leaders of the
Tougaloo contingent that sought to integrate Millsaps and Jackson's
commercial establishments, were almost killed in a suspicious
automobile accident. In the wake of these events, Eudora Welty
courageously published "Where Is the Voice Coming From?"—a
devastating portrait of the racist mindset.

Even before Welty's story was in print, her friend and agent
Diarmuid Russell expressed concern about violence in Jackson and about
Welty's safety. Welty, on the other hand, was afraid not for herself, but

for her mother. For months she had been consumed with anxiety about her mother's health and spirits, and that anxiety coupled with alarm for her mother in the local climate of hatred prevented Welty on one occasion from undertaking what would have implicitly been a symbolic act in support of integration. In late July 1963 (the time frame that seems most likely), she decided at the last minute, after much agonizing and with deep regret, not to be interviewed by Ralph Ellison on national television. She worried that a nationally televised appearance with this fellow writer, an African American man, would create a good deal of white hostility in Mississippi, hostility that she feared would be deflected from daughter to mother. She worried that such hostility would affect her ability to hire desperately needed caregivers for her mother, who in August was coming home from a five-month stint in a convalescent facility, and that it might affect the quality of care her mother would receive in the future. Although she and her mother had long been of one mind on the issue of civil rights, Welty sought to ensure that she alone would pay the price for their shared convictions. A desire to shelter her ailing mother from a volatile environment of racial tension and especially from white recrimination governed her decision, as she confided to Reynolds Price, not to be interviewed by Ellison. Ellison for a brief time was understandably mystified by Welty's decision. Shortly after the cancellation, Ellison told Price how open and outgoing Welty had always been with him, and he worried that he might have in some way unwittingly offended her. Price explained Welty's situation to him and also told Welty of Ellison's worries. According to Price, Welty then wrote to Ellison to explain her deep-seated apprehensions for her mother, and the Welty/Ellison friendship endured.[16]

Welty's relationship with the state of Mississippi, however, seemed in danger. On August 14, 1963, and again on August 28, she wrote her friend and former *Harper's Bazaar* fiction editor Mary Lou Aswell about the impossible, but desirable, prospect of moving her mother and herself away from Mississippi and its racist political leaders. And in the following spring, Welty continued to worry about the effect of social unrest upon her mother. In March 1964, she wrote to Aswell about her anxieties. She wanted, she wrote her old friend who had settled in Santa Fe, to move her mother to "some convalescent home in that part of the world." The fact that her mother was fifty miles away back in a Yazoo City nursing home, that Yazoo City was "reputed to be now the

headquarters of the Ku Klux Klan," that "our state is now authorized to
... arm the highway patrol," and that violence might prevent her from
reaching Yazoo City and her mother played heavily upon Welty's mind.
Recalling riots both black (Jacksonville, Florida) and white Oxford,
Mississippi), Welty wrote that she wanted to "bring my little mother to
some safe spot where she won't hear of this even."[17]

But Welty did not leave Mississippi or the South; neither did she
abandon a public stance in favor of an open society. Late in 1964, she
returned to the Millsaps College Christian Center, this time as the
college's writer-in-residence. Though she did not on this occasion have
to request unrestricted attendance—Millsaps now welcomed all to its
public events—she once again spoke during particularly tense times.[18]
The previous summer had seen the murders of three civil rights workers
in Philadelphia, Mississippi, the fire-bombing of forty black churches,
and the white Citizens' Council's intimidation of whites known to have
"moderate" sensibilities, intimidation that had not ceased.

In her December 2, 1964, lecture, titled "The Southern Writer
Today: An Interior Affair," Welty delivered comments that she would
later publish as "Must the Novelist Crusade?" Here, she ostensibly
rejected a political purpose for fiction, arguing that "there is absolutely
everything in great fiction but a clear answer," that fiction is concerned
more with the complexities of human experience than with proposing;
solutions to human difficulties. Welty followed the address with a
reading of "Keela, the Outcast Indian Maiden," which, appropriately,
examines the complexities of human relationships. The story describes a
crippled black man who was once kidnapped into carnival work as a geek
called Keela, the Outcast Indian Maiden, and who, notwithstanding the
horror of his past, feels nostalgic about the carnival experience, in which
he was noticed, as now within his own family he is not. The story further
deals with the guilt felt by Steve, the carnival barker, and with his
inability, nevertheless, to overcome the separation of race, and finally,
the story depicts a bystander's courting of detachment from the horror
and guilt Keela represents.

Complex though it is, however, "Keela" makes an important
political statement: the dehumanizing nature of racism is infinitely more
grotesque than a carnival sideshow. Certainly, Steve recognizes that by
acquiescing to this evil, he has become part of it: "'It's all me, see,' said
Steve. 'I know that. I was the one was the cause for it goin' on an' on an'

not bein' found out—such an awful thing. It was me, what I said out front through the megaphone.'" On the other hand, his acquaintance, Max, the owner of Max's Place, represses any guilt that might be his: "'Bud,' said Max, disengaging himself, 'I don't hear anything. I got a juke box, see, so I don't have to listen.'"[19] Max, in his disengaged state, might be speaking for many white Mississippians in 1964—they did not want to recognize their own complicity with evil, they did not want to accept the guilt they shared with Steve. But in reading this 1940 story to her 1964 audience, Eudora Welty called attention to that guilt. She did not ask that her audience become political activists, but she did ask, implicitly, that they refuse to be part of racist activities, that they recognize the humanity and complexity of all individuals. Millsaps College had already recognized the wisdom of positions like Welty's— within three months it announced that African American students were welcome to enroll at the college.

It is important to recognize that Welty's call for nonracist behavior was not a call to crusade, for she herself had chosen not to take to the streets. In a June 1965 letter to Mary Lou Aswell, Welty pondered her lack of stridency in the civil rights movement and concluded: "I'm to blame, I suppose, for not dashing into it and doing some of the shrieking, but I don't really think so, because it would not mean with me any change of heart. I've always felt as I do now, and I hope my feeling has been all the time in my work."[20] Welty's belief in the power of fiction was more important to her than public pronouncements. Even the aborted Ellison interview was to have focused on fiction, and certainly, in her public appearances at Millsaps, Welty had demonstrated how effectively her short stories expressed support for the civil rights movement.

As one who did not march on Washington, organize voter registration drives, or challenge Mississippi mores on national television, Welty continued to find meaningful ways to act against racism, speaking at the 1965 Southern Literary Festival, supporting interracial audiences and casts at New Stage Theatre from its planning stages in 1965 to the present day, describing the segregationists' benighted resistance to change as part of her 1966 story "The Demonstrators"—a story Jesse Jackson in a letter to the *New Yorker* praised as "true and powerful"—and inaugurating in 1967 a series of

Wednesday programs open to black and white at Jackson's St. Andrew's
Episcopal Cathedral.[21]

Welty's speech at the April 1965 Southern Literary Festival, held
in Oxford, Mississippi, in honor of William Faulkner, is particularly
instructive. Robert W. Hamblin has discussed the powerful statement
for civil rights implicit in Robert Penn Warren's festival address, an
address made twenty-four hours after a mob had harassed the Tougaloo
College delegation that had hoped to participate in the festival. Hamblin
might also have cited Welty's remarks, for they reiterated her faith in
fiction's power to expose and combat racist hatred. In the midst of a
wide-ranging discussion alluding to many Faulkner texts, Welty called
the audience's attention to the brutal murder of Joe Christmas, "waiting
with his hands in chains, 'bright and glittering,' ... as Percy Grimm
arrives with his automatic." Later she noted that Faulkner's characters
"are white, Negro, Indian, Chinese, Huguenot, Scotch, English,
Spanish, French, or any combination of these, and known always or at
any point of their time on earth from birth till death and in between."
And she added that these characters constitute "a population that has
reality as distinguished from *actuality*: they are our hearts made visible
and audible and above all dramatic; they are ourselves translated, and, at
times, transmogrified."[22] Welty thus suggested that race is as artificial a
concept as nationality and that to whatever race or nationality Faulkner's
characters belong, they represent our common humanity.

Such local actions were tremendously significant. As David
Chappell notes in his book *Inside Agitators: White Southerners in the Civil
Rights Movement*, white southerners who "were sickened by segregation"
together with white southerners who "found it terribly inconvenient in
practice" provided the civil rights movement with a strategic "moral and
political resource." Knowing of the existence of such whites, he writes,
"gave millions of black southerners; despite a dispiriting history of
crushed hopes and broken promises, confidence in their ability to win—
not simply confidence in the righteousness of their cause but in the
usually unrelated prospects of that cause for victory in the real world."[23]
Eudora Welty, one of those white southerners who was sickened by
segregation, thus played her own small but crucial and courageous role
in the move toward integration. By repeatedly refusing to comply with
racism in her private life and by locally encouraging others to refuse as
well, she became one of many who helped to create a climate for change
and for progress.

Most particularly, Eudora Welty had in her 1963 and 1964 Millsaps lecture/readings experienced the same sense of convergence that she had known in 1952. In 1952 she had found the fiction writer's values and the public domain pulled together, by Adlai Stevenson, and she actively supported the convergence he represented. In the sixties, however, Welty herself pulled the private and public together. She pulled together aesthetic and political concerns, stories from the past and contemporary conflicts, fiction and politics, and she sought to part the curtain that divided Mississippi's blacks and whites. Since that time, Welty's public political statements have been relatively few. For many years after William Winter's election as governor of Mississippi, Welty continued to sport a Winter bumper sticker on her car; in 1988 a full-page ad in the *New York Times* contained Eudora Welty's signature in support of the word *liberal*; and in 1992 a Clinton–Gore bumper sticker greeted those who knocked on her front door both before and long after election day. The convergence of public and private has continued to be a factor in Eudora Welty's life, but it was most ardently felt and acted upon in 1952 and 1963–64. For Welty, Stevenson's campaign for the presidency and the civil rights struggle of the sixties were causes that transcended the writer's need to be a "privileged observer."[24]

NOTES

1. Hubert Creekmore, "That Man Bilbo," *Time*, 22 October 1934, p. 2; Eudora Welty to John F. Robinson, Friday [November 1948], Eudora Welty Collection, Mississippi Department of Archives and History, Jackson.

2. "Bilbo and Rankin Get Blessings of Former Huey Long Chieftain," *Jackson Clarion Ledger*, 20 Dec. 1945; Walter Goodman, *The Committee* (New York: Farrar, Straus, and Giroux, 1968), 181; Eudora Welty, "Voice of the People," *Jackson Clarion-Ledger*, 28 December 1948.

3. James Loewen and Charles Sallis, *Mississippi Conflict and Change*, rev. ed. (New York: Pantheon Books, 1980), 239; Theodore Bilbo, cited ibid.; *Dictionary of American Biography*, s.v. "Rankin, John."

4. Eudora Welty, "What Stevenson Started," *New Republic*, 5 January 1953, 8; Eudora Welty, *One Writer's Beginnings* (Cambridge: Harvard University Press, 1984), 76, 102.

5. David Halberstam, *The Fifties* (New York: Villard Books, 1993), 236; Jean H. Baker, *The Stevensons* (New York: Norton, 1996, 323; Welty, "What Stevenson Started."

6. Baker, *Stevensons*, 333; Eudora Welty, "The Wanderers," in *The Collected Stories of Eudora Welty* (New York: Harcourt Brace, 1980), 452; Eudora Welty, "Writing and Analyzing a Story," in *The Eye of the Story: Selected Essays and Reviews* (New York: Random House, 1978, 114.

7. Baker, *Stevensons*, 325, 320.

8. Welty has discussed this and other biographical information with me in many conversations since I first met her in the summer of 1983.

9. Social Sciences Forum Announcements, Tougaloo College Archives, Tougaloo, Mississippi; John Quincy Adams, Papers and Audio Tapes, Faculty Papers, Series F, Millsaps College Archives, Jackson, Mississippi; Laura G. McKinley, "Millsaps College and the Mississippi Civil Rights Movement" (honors thesis, Millsaps College, 1989), 5–6; "Millsaps President and Wright Protest," *Jackson Clarion-Ledger*, 9 March 1958, section A; Jane Reid Petty and Patti Carr Black, conversations with the author, March 1997.

10. W.J. Cunningham, *Agony at Galloway* (Jackson: University Press of Mississippi, 980), 8.

11. Minutes of faculty meeting, 24 January 1963, Series B, Millsaps College Archives, Jackson, Mississippi; H.E. Finger Jr. Papers, Administrative Papers, Series A1, Millsaps College Archives, Jackson, Mississippi; Adams, Papers and Audio Tapes.

12. Eudora Welty, conversation with author, and R. Edwin King, conversations with author, 20 March 1997, 7 April 1997, 19 June 1997; Eudora Welty, "Words into Fiction," in *Eye of the Story*, 144, 145; Jerry DeLaughter, "Miss Welty Opens Literary Festival," *Jackson Clarion-Ledger*, 19 April 1963.

13. Eudora Welty, William E. Massey Lecture III, 6, Welty Collection, Mississippi Department of Archives and History, Jackson; Welty, *One Writer's Beginnings*, 101; Welty, "Powerhouse," in *A Curtain of Green* (New York: Harcourt Brace, 1941), 257.

14. Welty, "Powerhouse," 254, 265, 269.

15. John R. Salter, *Jackson, Mississippi* (Hicksville, N.Y.: Exposition Press, 1979), 102. Edwin King arranged for Moody to speak at Millsaps, attended the lecture with her, and told me of her comments about Welty's importance to the Tougaloo contingent (19 June 1997).

16. Diarmuid Russell to Eudora Welty, 17 June 1963, restricted papers, Welty Collection, Mississippi Department of Archives and History, Jackson. Welty's 1963 correspondence with Russell and with Mary Lou Aswell (restricted papers, Welty Collection, Mississippi Department of Archives and History, Jackson) suggests a late July decision by Welty; Reynolds Price, conversation with author, 25 October 1998. According to Price, the *Paris Review* intended to publish the interview with Ellison. Instead Hildegarde Dolson conducted the *Camera Three* television interview, and the *Paris Review* decided against publication. The interview aired on Sunday, August 18, 1963.

17. Eudora Welty to Mary Lou Aswell, 14 August 1963, 28 August 1963, [24/25 March 1964], restricted papers, Welty Collection quoted by permission of Eudora Welty.

18. Finger Papers, 9 August 1963. Sara Ann Weir covered this lecture for the Millsaps College paper. See "Miss Welty Tells Position of Southern Writers Today," *Purple and White*, 8 December 1964.

19. Eudora Welty, "Must the Novelist Crusade?" in *Eye of the Story*, 149; Eudora Welty, "Keela, the Outcast Indian Maiden," in *Curtain of Green*, 77.

20. Eudora Welty to Mary Louise Aswell, 8 June 1965, restricted papers, Welty Collection quoted by permission of Eudora Welty.

21. Tragic circumstances prevented Eudora Welty from being present on January 25, 1966, opening night at New Stage Theatre. Her mother died January 21 and her brother Edward, January 26. Although she could not attend the opening, which she had helped to make possible, Welty's public and private support far the theater never faltered and has continued to this day. In its early days, New Stage encountered white opposition to its racial policies. A bomb threat on opening night occurred even though no African Americans were in the cast; the fact that tickets were available for both blacks and whites, as Jane Reid Petty and Patti Carr Black told me in March 1997, was enough to generate the threat. (Both Petty and Black were among the founding members of the theater.) The theater continued its open-door policy nevertheless, and African Americans, though relatively few in number, were in its audiences from the inaugural year onward. The regular appearance of African Americans in casts began in 1969, making New Stage the first theater group in Mississippi "other than academic departments" to have both integrated audiences and casts (Martha H. Hammond, "Dialogue: New Stage Theatre and Jackson, Mississippi" [Ph.D. dissertation, University of Southern Mississippi, 1994], 196).

In 1970 when gunfire from the state highway patrol and the city police took two lives at Jackson State College, a black Jackson State student who was then a cast member of *The Ponder Heart* resolved to continue in her role, living with a white cast member for the run of the show (Hammond 181). Frank Hains, the director of the play, devoted a regular *Jackson Daily News* column to his deep sorrow at the violence that had just taken place, to the decision of Florence Roach to continue in her role, and to the play's relevance to this Jackson crisis. *The Ponder Heart*, he wrote, though it seems far removed from questions of "race relations or problems of the day," actually has "everything to do with them." This play, he continued, is "all about love and Uncle Daniel's unbounded love for all the world—and it's a reflection of the great love of humanity which lifts its author, Eudora Welty, into a state of grace few achieve on this earth." Hains thus proclaimed in print the role New Stage Theatre hoped to play in defining race relations, and human relations more generally, in terms of love, not hate and violence, and identified Eudora Welty as a person living and writing by such a code. See "On Stage—Eudora Welty's 'Ponder Heart': A Message of Love

Needed Now," *Jackson Daily News*, 17 May 1970, section C4. Welty sent Mary Lou Aswell a Xeroxed copy of Jackson's handwritten letter to the *New Yorker*, and this copy is included in the Aswell papers at the Mississippi Department of Archives and History.

In 1967 at St. Andrew's Cathedral, organizers wholeheartedly supported open admission to the series of readings, lectures, concerts, and plays, and they hoped African Americans would attend. As it turned out, however, Welty read to an all-white audience (personal conversation with Ann Morrison, chair of the 1967 Wednesdays at St. Andrew's programs, September 1999).

22. Robert W. Hamblin, "Robert Penn Warren at the 1965 Southern Literary Festival: A Personal Recollection," *Southern Literary Journal* 22 (Spring 1990, 53–62; Eudora Welty, untitled speech, p. 7, Southern Literary Festival, 23 April 1965, Welty Collection, Mississippi Department of Archives and History, Jackson, Mississippi.

23. David L. Chappell, *Inside Agitators: White Southerners in the Civil Rights Movement* (Baltimore: Johns Hopkins University Press, 1994), xxv.

24. Welty, *One Writer's Beginnings*, 21.

Chronology

1909	Eudora Alice Welty is born in Jackson, Mississippi on April 13 to Mary Chestina Andrews Welty and Christian Webb Welty.
1925	Graduates from Central High School, Jackson.
1925–27	Attends Mississippi State College for Women, Columbus.
1927–29	Attends University of Wisconsin, Madison; receives B.A. in English.
1930–31	Studies advertising at Columbia Graduate School of Business, New York City.
1931–34	Death of father; returns to Jackson to live; works part-time for local radio station, takes freelance jobs as newspaper correspondent and publicist.
1935–36	Works as a publicity agent for the WPA in Mississippi.
1936	Publishes "Death of a Traveling Salesman" in *Manuscript*; exhibits photographs in one-woman show in Lugene Gallery, New York City.
1937	Publishes "A Piece of News" and "A Memory" in the *Southern Review*.
1939	Meets Katherine Anne Porter.
1940	Diarmuid Russell becomes Welty's literary agent; attends Bread Loaf Writer's Conference.
1941	Spends summer at Yaddo Writers' Colony; *A Curtain of Green* is published, with introduction by Katherine Anne Porter; O. Henry Award, second prize, for "A Worn Path."

1942	*The Robber Bridegroom* is published; O. Henry first prize for "The Wide Net;" awarded Guggenheim Fellowship.
1943	*The Wide Net and Other Stories* is published; O. Henry Award, first prize for "Livvie is Back."
1944	Receives the American Academy of Arts and Letters award for $1000; moves to New York and works for 6 months for *New York Times Book Review*.
1946	*Delta Wedding* is published; stays 5 months in San Francisco visiting John Robinson.
1947	Gives lecture "The Reading and Writing of Short Stories" at writers' conference, University of Washington, Seattle; returns to San Francisco from August–November.
1949	*The Golden Apples* is published; wins Guggenheim Fellowship; travels to Europe: France, Italy, England, Ireland; meets Elizabeth Bowen.
1951	Visits England, and stays with Elizabeth Bowen in Ireland.
1952	Election to National Institute of Arts and Letters.
1954	*The Ponder Heart* and *Selected Stories* (Modern Library edition) is published; returns to Europe from July–October; gives lecture "Place in Fiction," at Cambridge University; receives Honorary LL.D. degree from the University of Wisconsin.
1955	*Bride of the Innisfallen* is published—last book for fifteen years; mother's eye surgery in March; receives William Dean Howells Medal of the Academy of Arts and Letters for *The Ponder Heart*.
1956	Attends Broadway opening of Chodorov-Fields production of *The Ponder Heart* in February; show runs until late June; receives Honorary LL.D. from Smith College.
1958–61	Receives the Lucy Donnelley Fellowship Award from Bryn Mawr College; becomes Honorary Consultant of the Library of Congress; illnesses of mother and brother, Walter, who dies in January 1959.
1964	Publishes *The Shoe Bird*, a book for children; accepts teaching post at Millsaps College.

1966	Death of mother in January; unexpected death of brother Edward a few days later.
1968	Wins O. Henry first prize for "The Demonstrators."
1969	"The Optimist's Daughter" is published in *The New Yorker*.
1970	*Losing Battles* is published; is awarded the Edward McDowell Medal.
1971	*One Time, One Place: Mississippi in the Depression, A Snapshot Album* is published with an introduction by Welty; named to American Academy of Arts and Letters.
1972	*The Optimist's Daughter* is published; wins Gold Medal for the Novel, National Institute of Arts and Letters; appointed to 6 year term on the National Council for the Arts.
1973	Wins Pulitzer Prize for *The Optimist's Daughter*; Diarmuid Russell dies.
1978	*The Eye of the Story: Selected Essays and Reviews* is published.
1979	Goes to England for artist-in-residence program at University College, Oxford.
1980	*The Collected Stories of Eudora Welty* is published.
1981	Awarded National Medal of Literature and Medal of Freedom.
1983	William E. Massey lecture series delivered at Harvard University in April.
1984	*One Writer's Beginnings*; Modern Language Association Commonwealth Award.
1985	Receives the American Association of University Women Achievement Award.
1986	Jackson Public Library named in honor of Eudora Welty; National Medal of Arts.
1987	Named Chevalier de L'ordre d'Arts et Lettres (France).
1989	*Photographs* is published; portrait of Welty added to National Portrait Gallery of the Smithsonian Institution.

1991   *Norton Book for Friendship*, eds. Eudora Welty and
             Ronald A. Sharp, is published; National Book
             Foundation Medal; Helmerich Distinguished Author
             Award; Cleanth Brooks Medal (Southern Letters);
             Eudora Welty Society organized.

1992   Awarded the Frankel Prize by the National
             Endowment for the Humanities.

1993   Receives PEN/Malamud Award (excellence in the
             short story); honorary doctorate, University of Dijon
             (France).

1994   *A Writer's Eye: Collected Book Reviews*, ed. Pearl Amelia
             McHaney, published.

1995   Eudora Welty Writers' Center established by
             Mississippi legislature on site of Welty's childhood
             home, 741 N. Congress St. in Jackson.

1996   Inducted into France's Legion of Honor.

1998   *Eudora Welty: Complete Novels* and *Eudora Welty: Stories,
             Essays, and Memoir* published as part of Library of
             America series.

2001   Dies on July 23.

Works by Eudora Welty

A Curtain of Green, and Other Stories, 1941.

The Robber Bridegroom, 1942.

The Wide Net, and Other Stories, 1943.

Delta Wedding, 1946.

The Golden Apples, 1949.

Selected Stories of Eudora Welty, 1954.

The Ponder Heart, 1954.

The Bride of the Innisfallen, and Other Stories, 1955.

Place in Fiction (essay; limited edition), 1957.

The Shoe Bird. (children's story), 1964.

Thirteen Stories. Ed. Ruth Vande Kieft, 1965.

Losing Battles, 1970.

One Time, One Place: Mississippi in the Depression, A Snapshot Album, 1971.

The Optimist's Daughter, 1972.

The Eye of the Story: Selected Essays and Reviews, 1978.

The Collected Stories of Eudora Welty, 1980.

One Writer's Beginnings, 1984.

Conversations with Eudora Welty. Ed. Peggy Prenshaw, 1984.

Photographs, 1989.

Norton Book of Friendship. Ed. Ronald A. Sharp and Eudora Welty, 1991.

A Writer's Eye: Collected Book Reviews. Ed. Pearl Amelia McHaney, 1994.

More Conversations with Eudora Welty. Ed. Peggy Prenshaw, 1996.

Eudora Welty: Complete Novels. Eds. Richard Ford and Michael Kreyling, 1998.

Eudora Welty: Stories, Essays, and Memoir. Eds. Richard Ford and Michael Kreyling. 1998.

Works about Eudora Welty

Bloom, Harold, ed. *Major Short Story Writers: Eudora Welty*. NY: Chelsea House, 1999.

———. *Modern Critical Views: Eudora Welty*. NY: Chelsea House, 1986.

Bowen, Elizabeth. "The Golden Apples." In *Seven Winters: Memories of a Dublin Childhood & Afterthought: Pieces on Writing*, ed. Elizabeth Bowen. NY: Alfred A. Knopf, 1962: 215–18.

Brinkmeyer, Robert H., Jr. "An Openness to Otherness: The Imaginative Vision of Eudora Welty." *Southern Literary Journal* 22.2 (Spring 1988): 69–80.

Carson, Barbara H. *Eudora Welty: Two Pictures at Once in Her Frame*. Troy, NY: Whitston, 1992.

Desmond, John F., ed. *A Still Moment: Essays on the Art of Eudora Welty*. Metuchen, N.J.: Scarecrow Press, 1979.

Devlin, Albert J. *Welty: A Life in Literature*. Jackson: UP of Mississippi, 1987.

Evans, Elizabeth. *Eudora Welty*. New York: Ungar, 1981.

Gretlund, Jan-Norby., and Karl Westarp. eds. *The Late Novels of Eudora Welty*. Columbia, SC: U of South Carolina Press, 1998.

Gygax, Franziska. *Serious Daring from Within: Narrative Strategies in Eudora Welty's Novels*. NY: Greenwood Press, 1990.

Hanson, Susan. *Eudora Welty and Virginia Woolf: Gender, Genre, and Influence*. Baton Rouge: Louisiana State University Press, 1997.

Johnston, Carol Ann. *Eudora Welty: A Study of the Short Fiction*. NY: Twayne, 1997.

Kreyling, Michael. *Author and Agent: Eudora Welty and Diarmuid Russell.* NY: Farrar, Straus & Giroux, 1991.

Manning, Carol S. *With Ears Opening Like Morning Glories: Eudora Welty and the Love of Storytelling.* Westport, Conn.: Greenwood Press, 1985.

Marrs, Suzanne. *One Writer's Imagination: the Fiction of Eudora Welty.* Louisiana State University Press, 2002.

Mississippi Quarterly 26 (Fall 1971). Special Eudora Welty issue.

Oats, Joyce Carol. "The Art of Eudora Welty." *Shenandoah*, XX (1969): 54–57.

Peterman, Gina D. "*A Curtain of Green:* Eudora Welty's Auspicious Beginning." *Mississippi Quarterly* 46 (Winter 1992–1993): 91–114.

Pollack, Harriet, and Suzanne Marrs, eds. *Eudora Welty and Politics: Did the Writer Crusade?* Baton Rouge: Louisiana State University Press, 2001.

Prenshaw, Peggy W. *Eudora Welty: Critical Essays.* Jackson: University Press of Mississippi, 1979.

Randisi, Jennifer L. *A Tissue of Lies: Eudora Welty and the Southern Romance.* Washington, D.C.: UP of America, 1982.

Schmidt, Peter. *The Heart of the Story: Eudora Welty's Short Fiction.* Jackson: University Press of Mississippi, 1991.

Trouard, Dawn, ed. *Eudora Welty: Eye of the Storyteller.* Kent, OH: Kent State UP, 1989.

Turner, W. Craig and Lee Emling Harding, eds. *Critical Essays on Eudora Welty.* Boston: G.K. Hall, 1989.

Vande-Keift, Ruth M. *Eudora Welty.* Boston: Twayne Publishers, 1987.

Waldron, Ann. *Eudora: A Writer's Life.* NY: Doubleday, 1998.

Warren, Robert Penn. "The Love and the Separateness in Miss Welty." *Kenyon Review* 6 (Spring 1944): 244–59.

Weston, Ruth D. *Gothic Traditions and Narrative Techniques in the Fiction of Eudora Welty.* Baton Rouge: Louisiana State UP, 1994.

WEBSITES:

Eudora Welty Newsletter
http://www.gsu.edu/~wwwewn/index.htm

The Eudora Welty Foundation
http://www.eudorawelty.org/

The Mississippi Writer's Page
http://www.olemiss.edu/mwp/dir/welty_eudora/index.html

Contributors

HAROLD BLOOM is Sterling Professor of the Humanities at Yale University and Henry W. and Albert A. Berg Professor of English at the New York University Graduate School. He is the author of over 20 books, including *Shelley's Mythmaking* (1959), *The Visionary Company* (1961), *Blake's Apocalypse* (1963), *Yeats* (1970), *A Map of Misreading* (1975), *Kabbalah and Criticism* (1975), *Agon: Toward a Theory of Revisionism* (1982), *The American Religion* (1992), *The Western Canon* (1994), and *Omens of Millennium: The Gnosis of Angels, Dreams, and Resurrection* (1996). *The Anxiety of Influence* (1973) sets forth Professor Bloom's provocative theory of the literary relationships between the great writers and their predecessors. His most recent books include *Shakespeare: The Invention of the Human* (1998), a 1998 National Book Award finalist, *How to Read and Why* (2000), *Genius: A Mosaic of One Hundred Exemplary Creative Minds* (2002), and *Hamlet: Poem Unlimited* (2003). In 1999, Professor Bloom received the prestigious American Academy of Arts and Letters Gold Medal for Criticism, and in 2002 he received the Catalonia International Prize.

AMY SICKELS is a writer living in New York City. She received her Master of Fine Arts in Creative Writing from Penn State University.

SAMUEL ARKIN has been a student in the English department at Yale University. He has also written on Christina Rossetti for the Bloom's Major Poets series.

In addition to his work on EUDORA WELTY, William M. Jones has edited *The Present State of Scholarship in Sixteenth Century Literature*.

HARRIET POLLACK is Associate Professor of English and on the advisory board of the Women's and Gender Studies Program at Bucknell University. She has also published "Photographic Convention and Story Composition: Eudora Welty's Use of Detail, Plot, Genre and Expectation From 'A Worn Path' Through Bride of The Innisfallen," which won the 1998 Kirby Award from the South Central Modern Language Association.

SUZANNE MARRS is Professor of English and the Welty Foundation Scholar in Residence at Millsaps College. She has also published *One Writer's Imagination: the Fiction of Eudora Welty*, which was named *Choice* Outstanding Academic Title.

INDEX

171